WINNIE MANDELA
Mother of a Nation

WINNIE MANDELA

Mother of a Nation

by

NANCY HARRISON

LONDON
VICTOR GOLLANCZ LTD
1985

First published in Great Britain 1985
by Victor Gollancz Ltd,
14 Henrietta Street, London WC2E 8QJ

British Library Cataloguing in Publication Data
Harrison, Nancy
  Winnie Mandela: mother of a nation.
  1. Mandela, Winnie   2. Black nationalism—
South Africa—Biography
  I. Title
  322.4'4'0924   DT 779.95.M3

ISBN 0–575–03657–5

Po
7/6/85
£8.95.

Photoset in Great Britain by
Rowland Phototypesetting Ltd, Bury St Edmunds, Suffolk
and printed by St Edmundsbury Press
Bury St Edmunds, Suffolk

In memory of my brother,
Bruce Silburn,
killed fighting with the Italian partisans
after he escaped from a p.o.w. camp,
Easter, 1944.

List of Illustrations

following page 90

Winnie arriving at court in the early sixties (*photo I.D.A.F.*)

Wedding day smiles (*photo Eli Weinberg/I.D.A.F.*)

Winnie and Nelson after his release from detention following the Sharpeville massacre (*photo I.D.A.F.*)

Winnie at home in Soweto with her two children (*photo Eli Weinberg/ I.D.A.F.*)

Her home in Soweto showing the protective wall

Winnie with Paramount Chief Sabata Dalindyebo (*photo Drum*)

Outside the Brandfort house, soon after arrival

Winnie with her grandchildren in the garden she created at Brandfort (*photo Nancy Harrison*)

Adelaide Tambo with Winnie's daughter, Zeni

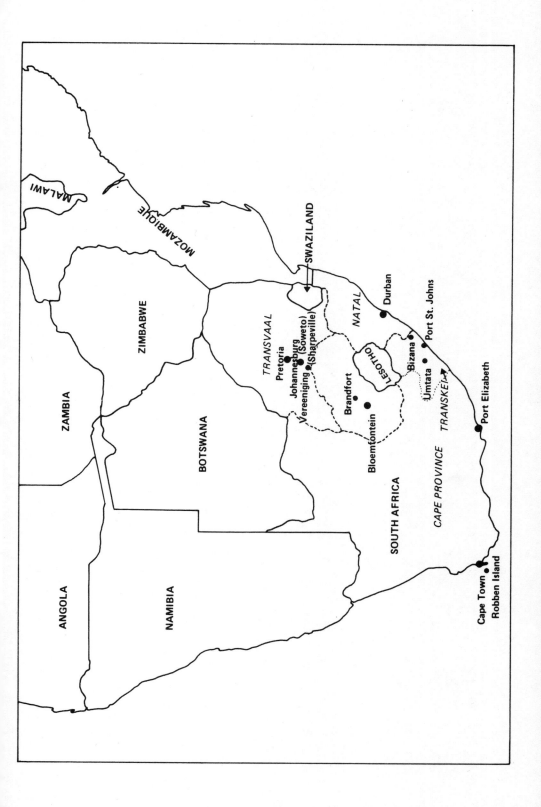

WINNIE MANDELA
Mother of a Nation

Prologue

THE SOUTH AFRICAN police colonel flung a piece of paper in her face. "This is the end of the road for you, Winnie Mandela. This time we are going to make you pay in a way you will never forget. From now on you are going to live in Brandfort till you die."

With incredulity she read the paper authorizing her banishment. She had never heard of Brandfort and had no idea where it was but she realized that the government, having failed in all its previous efforts to curb her influence, had devised this new punishment to circumvent the courts and silence the wife of Nelson Mandela. Defiantly she gazed back at the colonel—determined she would never give him the satisfaction of seeing her composure crumble. No sign of the shock she felt showed in her face nor was there any change in the erect, imperious posture.

For nearly 20 years she had endured bannings, house arrest, jail, detention without trial, constant surveillance and several attempts on her life. Her husband had been sentenced to life imprisonment, her children persecuted, her friends harassed. Yet all that had failed to scare her into abandoning her ideal of a just South Africa in which blacks and whites would be equally free to enjoy the land of their birth.

In the police station that cold, wintry morning Winnie was marshalling all her resources to disguise her dismay at being dragged, without warning, from her friends, her home, her work and her people in the sprawling township of Soweto, home of a million blacks. The government was confident that she would soon be forgotten as she languished in the middle of nowhere among strangers whose language she did not speak. The reality was to be just the opposite. Mercifully she was unaware of the ordeal ahead, but neither did the South African government have any inkling of how its scheme would misfire. Instead of sending her into obscurity they were focusing world attention on a figure hitherto little known outside her own country.

It might be a long, hard road to Brandfort in the sparsely populated Orange Free State, but it was far from the end of the road for Winnie Mandela, once a barefoot little girl in the Pondoland hills.

Chapter One

COLUMBUS MADIKIZELA STOOD shading his eyes against the sun as he watched the car jolt along the winding track. In these almost inaccessible Pondoland hills, where the normal modes of travel were on horseback or on foot, a motor car was still a novelty to the pupils of eMbongweni Primary School. They waited patiently for their headmaster to give them the signal to disperse but Columbus would make no move until the car had disappeared in a spiral of dust. He was an aloof figure—tall and imposing—his stern face disguising an innate kindness that endeared him to his pupils. They gazed at him speculatively, wondering whether his anger had abated. Sensing their concern Columbus smiled reassuringly and dismissed them to play. But he was still seething with anger: not at the children but at the two Afrikaner school inspectors who had just departed.

Every year at this time they came from the Cape Education Department, ostensibly to examine and advise, but it seemed to Columbus they were simply bent on criticizing headmaster and pupils alike. This time had been no exception. Almost before they had alighted from their official car, hot and irascible, they had complained that the little herd-boys had been too slow in chasing the cattle off the road. That comment had seemed to set the tone for their visit.

Columbus had hoped to persuade the inspectors how necessary it was to provide some basic facilities for his overcrowded and ill-equipped school. Classrooms were empty circular huts where the pupils were crammed right up to the doors with scarcely room to sit on the cowdung-smeared floors. "We do not even have desks and chairs," Columbus had pointed out. "Our only equipment is blackboard and chalk. And look at the overcrowding. Could your white children do good work under such primitive conditions?"

One of the inspectors had remarked that the children were lucky to be getting any education at all in this out of the way place. That remark had incensed Columbus. Normally a quietly spoken, dignified figure, he had

13

raised his voice and, ticking off the items on his fingers, had pointed out the discrepancies:

"White children have free schooling, free stationery, fine buildings, up-to-date equipment and compulsory education for all, but we blacks must provide everything ourselves and few of the parents can afford to do so. AND they must pay school fees for the privilege of sitting on the floor to learn. Is that justice?" he had asked heatedly.

His words, however, had only served to make the inspectors more hostile. They did not like "kaffirs" to give themselves airs and complain about the system. But Columbus had felt justified in making his protest. After all, he was a man of some influence in the community and the people expected him to speak up on their behalf. He represented Eastern Pondoland in the Bunga—the territorial council that met in Umtata to pass tribal laws for the whole of the Transkei—and he acted as interpreter when the tribal courts were held at the Great Place. The South African government insisted on white magistrates presiding at those courts so they needed Columbus, who was fluent in both English and Xhosa, to translate the proceedings. He had renounced the offer of a chieftainship to teach. Some of the tribal elders had doubted the wisdom of that but Columbus had no regrets. He found fulfilment in his teaching and in spite of, or perhaps because of, all the frustrations and lack of interest by the Education Department he was determined that his pupils should do well.

It was a source of great pride to him that at least three of his own children showed exceptional promise. His eldest son, Christopher (who was to become a headmaster like his father), was already doing well at boarding school, and Christopher's little brother, Lungile, was sharp beyond his years. But a man expected his sons to do well. It was his daughter, Nomzamo Winnie, who was the big surprise. Columbus smiled to himself as he remembered the astonishment on the faces of the Afrikaner inspectors when he had called eight-year-old Winnie up for questioning by them and she had replied so confidently in the English and Arithmetic oral examinations without a single error. They did not know she was his own child either, as all the children in his school bore the name Madikizela. The inspectors had laughed derisively at that, not understanding the system of the extended family in the Transkei. Sons brought their wives back to the family home, and when a kraal became overcrowded a section broke away to form another settlement. In Pondoland six of the 26 settlements or "locations" grouped together to form the Bizana district, were made up entirely of Madikizelas. The Pondo family unit being such a close one all his pupils were "family" to Columbus and they, in turn, regarded him with reverential awe. Stern though he was, he never found the need to resort to corporal punishment.

He watched the children as, released from the tension of the inspectors' visit, they shouted and fought in the playground. Few of them could afford the khaki shirts that were supposed to be the school uniform but, no matter how poor they might be, they all arrived at school with shiny faces and clean, if shabby and often incongruous, clothing. There would be no more school that day—he would leave them to their games.

Columbus smiled at the thought of how enraged the inspectors would be if they knew that he used his history classes to contradict some of the statements in the history books prescribed by the whites. Those books told only one side of the story—much of it simply untrue. Columbus made sure that every child in his care knew the other side and the true story of their heritage.

History was his great passion. On special days he would gather all the children together in the shade of an enormous wild fig tree and, always beginning with a wide sweep of the arm, as though to cast the imagination of his little listeners to the timeless valleys beyond, would tell them what had happened to their country and their people over the years. He would recount the epic story of the nine Xhosa wars against the white invaders—telling how thousands of fearless warriors had braved the bullets with only spears to defend the land they had lived in for centuries. He would explain that the black leaders depicted in the white history books as savage barbarians had, in fact, been brilliant and heroic generals. Sometimes when he described the injustices suffered by their people he would be so overcome with emotion that he had to leave the class to recover his equilibrium.

The shouts of the children roused him from his reverie. Columbus closed the door of the one-roomed stone schoolhouse that served as his office and set off for home. As he walked through the playground he noticed Winnie in the midst of a brawling group and smiled at the contradiction in her nature. In the classroom she seemed such a shy, submissive little thing but outside she became a real tomboy. Laughing boisterously, she would fight the boys, lead her shadow—her elder sister, Nancy—into mischief and lay down the law with an incipient imperiousness she was to develop later in life.

She was a caring child, too, mused Columbus, and not above wheedling things out of him when occasion demanded. When some of her classmates had dropped out of school Winnie alone had wanted to know why. He had explained to her the policy of the Education Department that required him to expel pupils whose parents could not afford to pay the fees. Winnie had been appalled because he and her mother had impressed upon all their children the necessity for education if they were to get anywhere in life. Winnie had pestered him to bring her classmates back until he had agreed to pay the fees himself from his meagre salary and re-admit the children. "After all," he consoled himself, "it is the young ones who must change the system and if they are to succeed a thorough education is imperative."

He knew it would not be easy to right the injustices suffered by the blacks and often he would lie awake at night pondering what the cost of such change would be. Gertrude, his wife, was another worry. He could see she was ailing. When their eldest daughter, Viyelwa, had come home to the umzi (homestead) from boarding school with the dreaded tuberculosis Gertrude had nursed her night and day. But the child died and now Gertrude had caught the disease. She would not be long for this world.

Gertrude had been a teacher, too, when he married her—the first domestic science teacher in the Bizana district. She had trained at Marianhill Roman Catholic Mission at Pinetown, outside Durban in Natal, though she herself was a staunch Methodist. Regarded in her youth as the local beauty and a great trend-setter, she was now a strict disciplinarian in the home and almost fanatically religious. She made her children pray three times a day and maintain rigid standards of cleanliness and order in the home. They were lined up each evening for inspection to make sure they had washed properly. Teeth cleaning was a particular ordeal, for they had to rub their teeth with ash until the gums bled.

Winnie was the fifth child of Columbus and Gertrude. She had been called Nomzamo which means, prophetically, as it transpired, "she who strives." The name Winnie was added for her christening in the Methodist Church. South Africa was still part of the British Empire and its people subjects of the King when Winnie was born on 26 September 1936. There is no written record of that event because there was no compulsory registration of black births in what was considered one of the most backward and undeveloped areas of South Africa. Undeveloped it certainly was, but with the existence of several mission schools in

Pondoland a number of the young blacks were being educated, though there was scant opportunity to make practical use of their learning. The word apartheid had not yet been coined nor its laws entrenched in the statute book, but blacks were very much a deprived and oppressed section of the population.

In the early days the arrival of the missionaries and traders in the Transkei had been followed by white farmers who wanted the labour, the land and the cattle of the blacks. The soldiers sent in to support the settlers had vastly superior weapons and equipment but it was only after almost a century of bitter and bloody warfare that the Xhosa-speaking people were subdued and, ultimately, impoverished. With the discovery of diamonds and gold in the second half of the nineteenth century, the demand for cheap labour for the mines and developing industries became pressing. All over South Africa land was taken from the indigenous people; they were forced to pay taxes and to comply with a host of restrictions. To find the money for their taxes they were obliged to become migrant labourers and this, with other intrusions, soon disturbed their way of life. It was to this legacy of a disrupted society, of enforced poverty, racial subjugation and of rural isolation that Winnie was born.

Her childhood home is close to the border with Natal and only three hours' drive from the packed beaches of the modern city of Durban. Yet at that time it was still remote, many of its settlements in the hills virtually untouched by western civilization, its afforested Wild Coast still as wild and free as its name implies.

The Transkei, with a population of two million blacks, is about the size of Switzerland and nestles between the mountains and the sea. In spite of its isolated situation it is an important source of black labour for the industries of South Africa. At that time it was known as a Native Reserve, which meant that it was intended for use only by the blacks living there—but that was in theory only. By the time of Winnie's birth, Port St Johns, annexed by the whites the previous century, had been developed as a coastal resort for whites; a road had been built through the Transkei connecting the Cape Province and Natal; whites had established little towns in the countryside, opened trading stores and cafés; they were farming fertile lands that the blacks had long regarded as their own and manning government offices and police posts. White officials were administering the white man's laws which overrode the customs of the indigenous people.

Though she likes to regard her early life as that of a typical barefoot

17

peasant girl, Winnie's upbringing, while spartan, was more privileged than most in the area. Her parents were better educated than many Transkeians and her father's activities as headmaster and Bunga councillor assured him of the deference of the community. In addition, he was a highly successful farmer in a culture where agriculture was paramount.

While most of the tribesmen in the rural areas wore colourful blankets Columbus, because of his position, always dressed in a suit. In those days the suits were shabby but beautifully pressed by Gertrude who also kept his frayed shirts neatly darned and the white collars starched. Though a kindly man who loved his children dearly, Columbus seemed unable to throw off his stern air of aloofness after school hours. The aura of authority, which his formal clothes seemed to emphasize, never left him, and even in his home his own children would rise when he entered a room and stand at attention till he left. They seldom addressed him unless their mother was present. There were no fatherly hugs and kisses but a great deal of his time was devoted to his children who seemed to realize that his stern admonitions were a symbol of his regard for them. Among his daughters only Winnie seemed able to get close to him—made possible, she believes, by her prowess in the classroom.

Gertrude, as a fervent Methodist, impressed upon her children the need to base their lives on Christian principles as opposed to the cult of the witch-doctors who were still dominant figures among the Xhosa. That early indoctrination against tribal superstitions and sorcery was to cause Winnie much confusion and heart-searching in later years when faced with the cultural clash between the age-old rituals and the ways of the western world. But until she was nearly nine there was no cloud on her horizon. Her home was a collection of eight picturesque grass-roofed huts and a T-shaped brick building in which Columbus slept. As a Christian Columbus was monogamous, but Winnie's grandfather had had 29 wives and so many children that till she was twelve and went away to school Winnie was unaware that there were people in the land with a different surname to hers.

There were always 20 to 30 children in her extended family household of three generations which included a number of waifs whom Columbus took in when their parents could not afford to feed them. At mealtimes they ate from huge enamel dishes, between six and ten to each dish, graduating to individual plates as they grew older. Columbus kept the household supplied with fresh meat, milk and produce from his lands, thus enabling them to eat far better than if they had relied solely on his paltry salary from the Cape Education Department—a fraction of that paid to white teachers. There was always boiled meat with vegetables for midday dinner, but the evening meal was Winnie's favourite. It consisted of sour milk and mealie meal cooked dry to the consistency of gravel porridge, known as umphokogo. What made it special to Winnie was that it was eaten around huge log fires while the old men and women smoked their pipes and recounted wonderful tales to the children. The myriad of stars overhead seemed to lend magic to the night. Even today Winnie remembers how those fireside tales stirred her imagination and left her spellbound.

She heard stories of great conquests, of black legends and heroes, of the demons said to lurk in the nearby forest and of the Bushmen—great hunters and painters—who had inhabited the land until they were exterminated in the early part of this century. She heard how her people had been living in their south-east corner of Africa at the time the Portuguese explorers first landed on the coast for water when seeking a sea route to India. That was hundreds of years before Jan van Riebeeck established a settlement at the Cape for the Dutch East India Company in 1652. This conflicted with the white man's claim that the blacks had come down from the north at the same time as the whites had arrived.

Winnie's grandmother often regaled the children with tales of how the men with blue eyes, pale skins and long straight hair had first arrived in Pondoland, with a bible in one hand and a button (her word for money) in the other, to steal her people's cattle and destroy their customs. The old woman had never set eyes on a white man, but she spoke of whites so disparagingly that Winnie laughingly refers to her grandmother as the first racist she ever knew. Nevertheless her grandmother's resentment of the actions of the whites made a lasting impression on her listeners.

A recurring theme amid the story-telling was indignation at the government's seizure of the Pondos' land and cattle. Under the destocking laws they were being deprived of thousands of head of cattle. Cattle were the Pondos' wealth; taking away his beasts was real deprivation, and the injustice of those measures was widely condemned. The government's explanation was that the land was vastly over-stocked and the numbers of cattle must be cut down to avoid soil erosion and eradicate cattle disease. But the Pondos believed the explanation lay with the powerful white farmers who had cast covetous eyes on their lands and who wanted to obtain the cheap black labour that would be available only if the Pondos were without lands of their own to farm.

Winnie listened intently to all these stories. They had a tremendous impact on the child growing up in a rural community miles from anywhere and without radio, shops or even such a mundane facility as a bus. But it was Columbus who inspired her most. It was he who sowed in her mind the first seeds of resentment at the injustices suffered by blacks—a resentment that was to remain with her throughout her life. To the Xhosa-speaking child the father is a sacred quality—his word is never questioned—thus many of the views that Winnie holds today were inspired by that early awareness aroused by Columbus. It is often suggested that it was only her marriage to Nelson Mandela that spurred Winnie to political activism, but it was from her own roots that her dedication and commitment sprang. Columbus impressed upon her that the white man had stolen their country—something she has never forgotten. It was from his example, too, that she learnt to care about others.

At school Winnie was always top of her class. No doubt her progress was helped by the fact that Columbus owned hundreds of books, from Aesop's Fables to tomes on physiology and hygiene. Over the years Winnie read them all, developing a love of reading that helped immeasurably to fill the lonely hours in later life.

The Madikizela children ran barefoot till their teens and they shared in the daily chores, particularly of milking, before and after school. But it was a happy and carefree existence for a child. Visits to the nearest village of Bizana were rare because there was no form of public transport of any kind from eMbongweni. When Winnie and her siblings visited Bizana they did so on foot. The journey took them a day and a night—the little ones forcing themselves to stay the course till they arrived, utterly exhausted, at the home of their maternal grandparents at Ndunge, a kilometre outside Bizana. The only time the children felt deprived was on those rare trips when they would gaze wide-eyed at the goods in the general dealers' stores. Counters were piled high with blankets and bolts of cloth, sweets, combs, mirrors and hundreds of items hanging from the ceilings, unimagined luxuries, which there was no money to buy.

There was no packaged entertainment in those remote areas but the children were never at a loss to provide their own. Winnie's homestead was set amid rolling green hills. Cattle, sheep and goats grazed on the lush grass surrounded by dense thickets of wild fruits which the children loved to eat in preference to the cultivated fruit in their father's orchard. As far as the eye could see was just hill upon rolling hill with the clear blue sky above. After school, when Winnie tired of playing ball games with the boys, she would spend hours making clay toys and models of animals. These were baked in a rough but surprisingly effective kiln built by the bigger boys. The kiln came in useful, too, when they managed to catch and kill a stray chicken to roast in it. The boys laid traps for dassies and spring hares, but those were taken home for the pot. When she recalls her childhood Winnie conjures up the fresh smell of cowdung and clay in the sun-drenched dongas and the wonderful feeling as she raced across the undulating veld—exploring the countryside, living in a dream world close to the soil and, as yet, untroubled by the harsh discriminations endured by blacks in the cities.

Although eMbongweni is so remote Columbus, with his frequent visits to Umtata to sit on the Bunga, kept in touch with world affairs and saw that the tribespeople and his pupils knew what was going on elsewhere. During the war he gave them regular bulletins whenever he returned from his travels or from a ride on horseback into Bizana. The children loved to hear tales of the wicked Nazis and stories of the battles and bombings, though they found it hard to imagine what a bomb was like.

Even in that isolated corner of South Africa the effects of the war were considerable. Winnie remembers that almost overnight many of the young men seemed simply to disappear. Hundreds of them joined the white man's army. Much to their indignation they were not allowed to use or carry guns but were given smart uniforms in which they swaggered proudly when they returned home on leave before sailing for Egypt. Many of them were killed on active service. It was ironical that so many blacks rushed to volunteer in the fight against a foreign racist oppressor while at home oppression of their own people was to be even further accentuated in the years to come.

As the war progressed there were sudden shortages of foodstuffs the children had always taken for granted. Once there was no sugar for weeks on end and when soap became scarce this caused real hardship in Winnie's home, where both parents were fanatical about cleanliness and health. The children were put to work collecting a soapy herb from the hillsides—keeping a wary eye open for snakes in the long grass—and Gertrude used the herb to make a traditional soap called inqubebe.

Winnie's most vivid impression of those years came in 1945, towards

21

the end of the war. The children awoke one morning to the news that Gertrude had died. Winnie was not yet nine years old, and the trauma of those days returned in nightmares for a long time to come. For the next few days the children, bewildered and distressed, watched the preparations for the funeral of their mother who had been the pivot of their lives. The huts were washed down with black ochre and the windows smeared with white in mourning. When the whole district turned up for the funeral Winnie had never seen so many people together. Two oxen and several sheep were slaughtered to feed the mourners. Family elders sat with their heads bowed down near the cattle kraal while the women grouped together on the grass, talking in whispers, their shoulders covered with black shawls.

The Methodist Church service was held in the open air since no hut could hold so many people. Winnie and her siblings, the girls crying bitterly, sat beside the black-draped coffin on which lay Gertrude's neatly folded church uniform. (In South Africa black women belonging to Christian churches often adopt a uniform mode of dress when attending services.) Afterwards the coffin was carried to the family cemetery at the bottom of the garden where simple white crosses marked the graves. Winnie could not bear to look as her mother's coffin was lowered into the earth. She clung to Nancy, shivering with fear.

The youngest child was only a baby still and, although kindly relatives came in droves to help, the household was thrown into chaos without Gertrude's strict regime and discipline. Like his children Columbus was stricken by his loss, but when he recovered from his first grief he realized the turmoil which had enveloped the household. He decided he would bring up his children himself, a most unusual step for a Pondo father. The helper aunts were sent back to their own homes and gradually the household was restored to order, with each of the children taking on tasks for which their mother had trained them. Inevitably Columbus grew closer to his children, yet they still stood in awe of him. Winnie, though, recalls that she turned to him for advice on everything throughout her formative years.

When the war ended the momentous news was brought to eMbongweni by a man driving a lorry. "There are big celebrations going on in the streets and in the Town Hall in Bizana," he told them. The children begged permission for a lift back with him to join in the festivities. They climbed into the back of the lorry and throughout the journey chatted excitedly about this unexpected treat. But when they reached Bizana and rushed up to the Town Hall they found the doors barred to them. The celebrations were for whites only. To this day Winnie remembers the sickening disappointment she felt at being shut out on such a great occasion.

The children peered enviously through the Town Hall windows, watching bleakly as the beautifully dressed white children and their parents feasted lavishly, the sounds of merriment mingling with the rousing music of a band. To discourage the piccanins from looking in the windows some of the whites tossed oranges and sweets on to the ground outside while those less fortunate than they scrambled and fought to get one. To Winnie it was her first salutary lesson in what it meant to be black in South Africa. It gave her her first glimmer of understanding of her father's impassioned concern to right the injustices suffered by their people.

She realized very early, for her father kept impressing it upon her, that to get on in life she must be properly educated and able to speak fluent English. But when she was twelve and in the top class of Standard Six at her father's school her education came to an abrupt halt. Columbus called her in to the office one day.

"My child," he said, "I have bad news for you. I have had instruction from the Department to close down the Standard Six class right away because we are overcrowded. They are transferring these classes to secondary schools and in future we will go only as far as Standard Five." Winnie was stricken. In South Africa the school year begins in January and continues through to early December with breaks after each of four terms. The instruction came through in March when the first term of the new school year was drawing to a close. The older children in the family were already at schools in Bizana or the adjoining village of Ndunge, but Columbus explained to Winnie that those schools were full to overflowing and there was no room for her. Columbus might have been expected to take his daughter back into the Standard Five class but he did nothing of the sort. Perhaps he was testing her resilience.

Schooled in obedience, Winnie did not question her father's decision even though it meant that she now became a full-time worker on his lands. She fetched the cattle and sheep from the fields, milked cows, picked crops and even walked behind the oxen holding a heavy plough as the furrows were prepared for planting. And every day she walked a long way to a little stream called Ngongozayo to fetch a drum of water for household use. She carried this back balanced on her head—an art that is learnt early in life by all African girls in country areas. It was undoubtedly this routine exercise in her childhood that produced in Winnie her graceful posture and erect, swinging gait.

Winnie worked diligently at her chores, resigned to the fact that there was no distinction between the sexes when it came to hard work, though she never accepted that toiling as a farm labourer was to be her lot for ever. And when at last the winter days began lengthening, her faith was justified in a way she had never anticipated. One of her sisters was taken ill and was sent home from school. Columbus immediately entered Winnie to fill the vacancy. Her joy was unbounded. The new school was at Ndunge, which was too far to commute to each day, so her father arranged for her to stay during the school terms with her maternal grandparents who lived there.

Chapter Two

WINNIE'S FIRST DAY at her new school was in September—eight months after the rest of the children had begun the academic year. Classes were overcrowded and the facilities inadequate. Even though education was neither compulsory nor free, as it was for whites, many black parents were prepared to endure great hardship to pay for it.

In the Standard Six class at Ndunge there were 200 pupils divided into three groups. When Winnie took her place in the classroom she learnt, to her dismay, that they were about to write their revision tests for the end-of-year examinations. She was told to sit down and write too. After five months without schooling she did so with great trepidation, but was not too despondent when the results placed her 58th among the 72 in her group. She worked hard to catch up and two months later, when the class wrote the external Standard Six examination of the Cape Education Department—in those days the same as that written by white children—Winnie was one of only 22 who passed.

"It was a great moment. I will never forget my excitement," she says. "Against all the odds I had got through and could now go on to the Emfundisweni Secondary School in Bizana to take my Junior Certificate."

That was an unforgettable event, not least because it meant that Winnie would wear shoes for the very first time in her life. Clothes have always had a special appeal for her. Whether it be colourful beaded tribal dress, the long bright caftans she often favours or mannish khaki trousers and bush-shirt, she has a flair for dressing with great style and elegance. But no new garment has ever given her as much pleasure as that first pair of shoes which she pulled on to feet hardened and toughened by the stones of the veld.

Her father took her to Bizana to buy the shoes and the black and white uniform she was required to wear. At the time she was something of a tomboy. She was always wearing her brother's clothes at home so Columbus, to reward her for having done so well, bought her a man's overcoat in addition to her uniform. It was far too big for her, and the other children at Emfundisweni were to be convulsed with laughter every time they saw her in it. But Winnie did not care. She was accustomed to wearing clothes that were too big so as to allow her to grow into them: with money so tight each garment had to last a long time. The overcoat was her most treasured possession and she wore it through the winters for the next few years.

Her new garments carefully parcelled up, Winnie went with her father to a nearby store in the town to buy food. Like all shops in the village of Bizana it was run and owned by whites for black custom. That day it was filled with tribesmen wearing traditional colourful Pondo blankets that seemed to brighten the gloomy interior of the tin-roofed store.

Some of the tribesmen from the hills had ridden in, straight-backed, on their sturdy ponies; others had travelled long distances on foot, many accompanied by a wife with her baby on her back. It was not unusual for the journey to take them a day or more of walking to reach the trading posts. They would arrive dusty and tired, relieved to have reached their destination even though there was nowhere for them to relax in comfort and take some refreshment. There was not even an eating-house for blacks in Bizana nor any proper pavement where the travellers could sit down and rest. Those quiet, dignified men would converge in clusters in the street to exchange news and gossip before going about their business and setting off home again.

While Winnie waited for Columbus to be served she noticed a tribesman with his wife and baby buy a loaf of bread, some sugar and a soft drink. The trio seemed intensely weary and looked as though they had travelled a long way. The baby was yelling and the mother sank down on the floor in a corner of the shop and put the child to her breast to feed while the father squatted beside her and started breaking the dry loaf to appease their hunger. Suddenly there was a shout. A white youth who had been serving Columbus leapt across the counter and flew at the little family group in a rage. Viciously kicking at them and their food he screamed at them to get out: he would not have kaffirs soiling his shop.

Winnie was horrified. She had never before seen such unprovoked aggression. Surely someone would intervene? But the white boy's parents, owners of the shop, just laughed. Not a single black in the crowded store raised even a murmur. Winnie looked at her father appealingly. He was her teacher, always speaking out against wrong. He had taught her to respect the dignity of others and to have such pride in her race. Surely he would never allow a fellow Pondo to be humiliated in this way? But, though Columbus seemed to recoil with deep hurt, he said nothing. How could he turn a blind eye to such injustice? Years later Winnie was to realize that if he had intervened he would probably only have exacerbated the situation, but that day she could not understand his silence and remained puzzled and ashamed at the memory.

It left an indelible scar. It was a cloud in her carefree, youthful existence; her first experience of racial brutality; her first realization that it was wrong to stand aside and do nothing to right an injustice and the first niggling doubt about her father's infallibility.

Imperceptibly Winnie's character was taking shape. Her mother had set the strict moral code with her stern religious discipline; her father had instilled in her a fierce national pride with his tales of her heroic ancestors; and by his caring and helpful attitude towards the poor in their community he had demonstrated the virtue of compassion. Now the degrading incident in the store was the first of many racial affronts that were to harden her in the years to come.

But at that stage Winnie, a thirteen-year-old with a man's overcoat and treasured new shoes, was still an unsophisticated little country girl, wide-eyed and coltish, and eager to please her adored but austere father by doing well at her studies. She did. She passed her Junior Certificate with flying colours and when she took home the news of her success Columbus told her of his plans for her. For a long time he had been considering the best way of harnessing her undoubted ability and the concern she always displayed to others in need. When he read of a college in Johannesburg that was training black students to become social workers—the first and only one of its kind in South Africa—he knew he had found the answer. He was determined that Winnie should study there. Once qualified she would be able to help her own people in a constructive way. But first she would need a really good pass in the matriculation (university entrance) examination in order to qualify for admission to the college where places were much in demand by urban dwellers better able to afford the fees. So that she could study for her matriculation Columbus sent Winnie as a boarder to Shawbury High School at Qumbu, in the Transkei.

Shawbury was a Methodist Mission School. At that time there was a number of such schools run by various denominations throughout the Transkei. Most of them closed down later rather than conform to the restrictive practices and curricula introduced by the government for blacks as part of the Bantu Education Programme. But before that time many of Winnie's generation, both men and women, had progressed from the mission schools to make their mark in the South African liberation struggle. It was a great financial strain for Columbus to keep Winnie at boarding school. There were no scholarships for blacks at that time, no matter how bright they might be, but he was determined to give her the chance she deserved.

Since their mother's death the bond between Winnie and her older sister, Nancy, always a close one, had grown even stronger. Nancy shared her father's faith in Winnie's ability and, when she realized how hard it was for Columbus to finance her sister's education, she decided to leave school herself and try to do odd jobs at home so that she could send pocket money to Winnie. One of the jobs she undertook was the physically arduous one of stripping the bark from the wattle trees in her father's plantation to sell to a white man who regularly came round asking for it for use in shoe-making. He was from a tannery in Durban and was buying the wattle bark illegally, but the few pence he gave Nancy for each load provided her with the much-needed cash to send to Winnie for books and stationery at boarding school.

Nancy's motherly care of her and the sacrifices she made to help her sister were not forgotten by Winnie. Years later, as soon as she could afford to do so, she sent Nancy the fare to travel to Johannesburg and arranged for her to train at the Bridgeman Memorial Hospital where she qualified as a nursing sister.

Shawbury proved a new and enlightening experience for Winnie. She was a studious scholar, popular with her fellows, and in her final year she was elected head prefect of the school. The stories she had heard recounted at home had been mainly about the history and exploits of her ancestors and the ongoing land and cattle disputes with the government. Now, to her amazement, she learnt from her teachers what was happening to the working people in the cities.

The teachers at Shawbury were mostly graduates of Fort Hare University College which at that time was a hotbed of political activism. They were fiercely proud of their African origins, militant in spirit and determined that their pupils should know what the white government was doing to their people. This was an eventful time in South African politics. Winnie was at Shawbury in 1951 and 1952—the year of the Defiance Campaign against apartheid. The Nationalist government had been in power for four years under the premiership of the intractable racist, Dr D. F. Malan, an Afrikaner Calvinist minister. Already he had extended segregationist legislation as Afrikaner nationalism tightened its grip on the country.

Rumblings of black discontent over the vicious policies of the Nationalist government surfaced primarily through the African National Congress. This had been in existence since 1912—aimed at redressing grievances. But its moderately voiced pleas for reform had fallen on deaf ears. Then, in 1944, a group of young members more militantly inclined than the old guard started the Youth League of the ANC. They pressed for a programme of action to include strikes, stay-aways and national days of protest. The Youth League's plan was adopted by the ANC in 1949, and then in June 1952 they launched a massive civil disobedience scheme known as the Defiance Campaign.

That campaign did much to increase the alarm felt by whites, and white Afrikaners in particular, at the growing threat of articulate blacks. The ANC was pressing for the repeal of the hated pass laws, for the right to own land, for an end to influx control, for equal justice in the courts and, above all, for one man, one vote. Blacks had and still have no say in the government of the country in which they outnumber whites by five to one. News of the turbulence this defiance of unjust laws was creating in the cities filtered through to Shawbury pupils in their isolated school. When they heard anyone shouting that *Zonk* and *Drum* had arrived there was a rush to pounce on the latest copies of those two black magazines that dramatized each event in the campaign.

The pupils thrilled with pride to read that 8,500 volunteers, most of them black but with a few Indians and coloureds and a sprinkling of whites, had agreed to invite arrest by deliberately flouting the discriminatory laws. The papers described how the volunteers walked through the "Europeans Only" entrances at railway stations (a heinous crime in the eyes of many whites); stayed out after the sounding of the curfew designed to keep blacks off the streets at night; burnt their hated passes and entered locations (black ghettos) without a permit—this last being carried out by white supporters who normally were prohibited from entering without written permission. The news items emphasized that the acts of defiance in themselves were harmless and that there was no violence. Nevertheless the police arrested 8,000.

The man who planned the campaign with its code of discipline emphasizing non-violence was a young lawyer named Nelson Mandela. The girls had all heard of that great chief who was already a legendary figure to them. None of them, least of all Winnie, ever expected to meet him but they sang songs about him and other leaders whom they idolized. The African National Congress was venerated to such an extent that many of the girls worked themselves up into frenzies of admiration. Then they heard that Mandela had been arrested for attending a meeting in defiance of a banning order that the government had imposed on him to curb his movements and utterances.

In the isolated rural setting of Shawbury the pupils led sheltered lives and they had yet to come in contact with the daily insults of apartheid. But they pored over the tattered copies of *Zonk* and *Drum* and inflamed each other with suggestions of how they could help. They held a meeting at which they, too, decided to defy authority by going on strike against poor facilities and poor hostel conditions.

Winnie was in a dilemma. She was about to write the matriculation examination and, knowing what a sacrifice it had been for her father and Nancy to finance her education, she was determined to justify their confidence in her. She was head prefect of the school, too, and partly responsible for discipline. Though she sympathized with the would-be strikers and admired the efforts of the Defiance Campaigners, she claims she was still very much a schoolchild and did not properly understand the situation. The ring-leaders, many of them much older than fifteen-year-old Winnie, were determined to strike. Winnie decided to keep a low profile.

The "uprising" by the schoolchildren at Shawbury was widely reported throughout the country, with pictures splashed across the front pages of girls in gym-slips protesting. The white population, already on edge with the Defiance Campaign, was scandalized. That mere children could react in this fashion caused consternation among the authorities and brought swift retribution in the way of mass expulsions. Only those who were writing their final examinations and who were not the instigators were allowed to remain at Shawbury. All the others were told to return with their parents the next term when their re-admission would be considered. It was a worrying and upsetting time for Winnie. Nevertheless she managed to concentrate on her studies. Her diligence paid off for, in spite of the upheaval around her, she obtained a first-class pass in the matriculation examination.

Winnie is always thankful that she completed her schooling before the iniquitous Bantu Education Act came into force in 1954. It was designed to condition them to subservience by restricting the syllabuses and placing the emphasis on such pursuits as gardening, tree planting, woodwork, singing and handwork. By leaving little time for essential subjects it thus turned out people untrained for anything but menial labour. It was only one of many apartheid laws, covering almost the entire range of human relations, that were to be introduced by the government, entrenching policies that had been in operation for many years. In 1950 the people had been compartmentalized by the Population Registration Act which classified them as white, Cape Coloured, Malay, Griqua, Chinese, Indian, other Asian and other Coloured. The blacks—far and away the largest section of all—were fragmented into different ethnic groups in order to divide them rather than allow them to continue as one nation. To entrench apartheid the government was to introduce in the years ahead numerous laws, among them the Prohibition of Mixed Marriages Act, the Group Areas Act, the Native Labour Act and the Reservation of Separate Amenities Act. Further oppressive measures followed.

When Winnie arrived home again after sitting for her matriculation she found there was more to celebrate than the end of her schooldays because Columbus, who had been a widower for so long, had decided to marry again. His second wife was a spinster schoolmistress, Hilda Nophikela, with whom Winnie immediately developed a mother–daughter relationship that has endured throughout all vicissitudes to the present day. The only child of that marriage, Winnie's half-sister Zukiswa, now practising as a dental therapist at Butterworth Hospital in the Transkei, has also remained close to Winnie. Mother and daughter have made the long journey to Brandfort to visit Winnie on many occasions since her banishment.

31

Chapter Three

HER FATHER'S DREAM of Winnie becoming a social worker was about to be realized. She was still an unsophisticated country girl, though her appearance belied this. She had grown into a tall and slender sixteen-year-old with velvety smooth skin, good looks inherited from both parents and the graceful, erect carriage that marks black women raised in a rural area. But beneath her demure exterior lay a fiery nature. She was not above resorting to fisticuffs if necessary. "Some people need a good clout to knock sense into them," she would explain.

At that time Winnie had never been further than the dusty little one-horse villages of the Transkei. She had never even visited the white holiday resorts of Margate or Port Edward, just over the border and less than an hour's drive from Bizana, separated from the Native Reserve by the Umzimkulu River. In those days it was crossed by a manually operated ferry hauled on cables across the wide river by teams of black labourers. But Winnie had never been to the other side. All that she knew of the outside world she had gleaned from books, newspapers, her teachers and her father. The white people she had encountered could be numbered on the fingers of her hands. A move to South Africa's biggest city, therefore, was an awesome venture. "I was quite raw," she laughs.

Throughout the Christmas holidays Winnie made her preparations for the move. A constant stream of relatives called at the homestead with advice. Nancy, hand over her mouth to suppress the giggles, would come rushing to find her. "Two more aunties to see you," she would tell her sister and Winnie, composing her features, would go out to greet the elderly newcomers and sit gravely, eyes downcast, listening to the advice of older women who had never left the district but who wanted to warn her of the pitfalls awaiting the unwary in Egoli—the City of Gold—as Johannesburg is known.

The tribal elders were full of admonitions, too. She must never forget Pondoland—as if she could—and she must uphold the proud heritage of the Pondos and behave at all times as if the spirits of her ancestors were watching. Winnie was somewhat daunted by all the warnings and advice but Columbus assured her that she had nothing to fear as he had organized everything. He showed her the letters he had received in response to his own, ensuring that she would be cared for in Johannesburg. He had arranged for her to board at the Helping Hand Hostel in Hans Street, Jeppe, right in the heart of Johannesburg and a long way from the overcrowded locations where crime flourished in the atmosphere of depression.

The Helping Hand Hostel had been opened 40 years previously by the Congregationalist American Board to provide safe accommodation for young black women domestic workers who were often molested when they occupied the customary back-yard rooms at the white houses where they were employed. Over the years the character of the Hostel had changed as nurses, teachers and other educated working women, for whom there was nowhere else to stay, sought accommodation there. Eventually a section was reserved for black women students and it was from the safety of that haven that Winnie was to get to know Johannesburg. Throughout her stay efforts were made to force the Hostel authorities to move out of the white part of the city to the black townships, but these succeeded only many years after Winnie had left.

When Columbus took his daughter to the railhead to begin her journey it was the first time she had ever been on a station and the first time she would travel in a train. Concerned that on such a long journey a young girl would need protection from the rough types she might encounter on the trip Columbus handed his daughter into the care of two young tribesmen, Moses and Jeremiah, relatives who had tilled his lands for him and with whom he knew she would be safe. Moses and Jeremiah were going to Johannesburg, too. Only in their case it was to work as migrant labourers on the gold mines. Seventy per cent of Transkei men between the ages of fifteen and fifty-five endure all the social deprivation and hardship of the migrant system.

On boarding the train Winnie and her two escorts pushed their way into one of the crowded, dirty third-class carriages in which blacks were obliged to travel to segregate them from the comfortable compartments marked "Europeans Only". Finding an empty space on one of the hard, wooden seats, Winnie wedged herself in at the window. Eager hands passed up parcels of cooked mealies, fruit and bottles of cold tea for the journey. Only the carriages for whites served meals and refreshments—blacks had to provide their own or go without.

There were no tears from Winnie as she leant out of the window to wave an excited goodbye. Her father's reticent nature had bred in her a stoicism that was to serve her in good stead. She was certain of his love and care and trusted him implicitly but he remained an aloof, schoolmasterly figure who had never even hugged or kissed her. For many years Winnie's natural exuberance had been disguised beneath a seemingly shy and demure exterior—undoubtedly the result of her father's distant nature—but in Johannesburg she was to develop her outgoing personality without restraint. On the station platform only Nancy, who had mothered Winnie and shared her confidences and hopes, wept to see her favourite sister leave for the distant and dangerous metropolis of which they had heard so much. As the train slid out of the station Winnie's excitement ebbed and she sat, silent and subdued, awed at the thought of what lay ahead and what was expected of her.

Sensitive to her mood, her companions sought to distract her by telling her of their life on the mines. This was to be their second year away from home and it would be another year before they would see their families again for a brief respite. They told her how scared and apprehensive they had felt when first arriving at the mine and discovering the dreadful conditions under which they were expected to live.

"We stay in huge, men-only hostels in special compounds," said Moses, his expression deadened by the prospect. "It is terrible. There are twenty of us to a room. We sleep on concrete slabs and have to flatten cardboard boxes to put on the cement so the beds won't be so hard and cold." Jeremiah told Winnie there was no privacy at all. Men were fighting, drinking, cooking, talking, playing radios and mouth organs all the time so there was a constant noise as not everyone worked the same shifts. Their basic wage was only £5.16s. a month and they had to work eleven months to fulfil their contracts.

Winnie was disturbed by these tales. She had seen how disruptive the migrant labour system was to the lonely wives and children left behind to eke out a meagre living from the land unsupported by their menfolk. But she had not realized how hard life was for the men themselves on the mines. She thought she would write to her father to ask him to discourage Pondos from going to the mines; but what else could they do? The poverty in the Transkei was terrible and often the men had no other way of paying their compulsory tax than by becoming migrant workers. She knew some of the men were able to work closer to home in the sugar cane fields on the Natal South Coast but she had heard that, though the sugar planters were immensely wealthy men, they paid even poorer wages to their workers than the mines.

Moses and Jeremiah told Winnie they had attended school only as far as Standard Three and then only intermittently when their parents could afford the fees. For much of their young lives they had been tilling fields or herding cattle. Winnie was saddened at the thought of such promising young men facing a lifetime of lowly paid menial labour because they were black and had never had the chance to be educated—and she was furious at the cruel migrant labour system that parted families for a year at a time.

Eventually the train neared Johannesburg and the men pointed out to Winnie the huge sand-coloured outcrops on the flat landscape. "Mine dumps," they told her. "When the gold is taken out of the crushed rock they throw the slag remaining on to a heap and it piles up like a hill."

After the beautiful soft scenery of Pondoland Winnie thought the highveld around Johannesburg harsh and ugly. Little did she realize that before long she would be captivated by the place and unable to visualize living anywhere else.

Her two escorts had to join their contract boss as soon as the train arrived so Winnie said a hasty goodbye and stepped off the coach to stand bewildered among the noisy, jostling crowd. But it was not long before two smiling white women approached her.

"Winnie Madikizela?" asked one. Winnie, relieved to be recognized so soon, smiled her assent.

"Welcome to Johannesburg," added the other. She introduced herself as Mrs Phillips, wife of Professor Ray Phillips, head of the Jan Hofmeyr School of Social Work at which Winnie was to study, and her companion as Mrs Frieda Hough, whose husband was a lecturer and Field Work Director at the School.

"Johannesburg will seem a frightening place at first but you will find the other students very friendly and I am sure you will like the hostel where you are to stay," she said.

Winnie, impressed by their kindly manner which was in such marked contrast to the usual condescension of whites towards blacks, shook hands with the two women. Later she discovered that both were

Americans and not South Africans at all. Mrs Phillips, like her husband, was a missionary of the Congregational Church and Mrs Hough was the daughter of American missionaries and herself a social worker. She had married a fair-minded Afrikaner, Michiel Hough, who was later to become a professor and head of the sociology department of Fort Hare University.

The two women drove Winnie to the hostel that was to be her home for the next four and a half years. She had reached Johannesburg on a weekday morning and, early as her arrival had been, the streets of Johannesburg were already teeming with people. Winnie had never seen such crowds, such bustle and commotion, in her life! A stream of cars, buses and lorries, more than she could have believed possible, was already causing traffic jams on the wide roads and everywhere there were people, hordes of people, rushing hither and thither. She felt a mounting excitement—such beautiful cars, such magnificent buildings—already the vibrancy, the clamour and the haste of Johannesburg were affecting her.

Mrs Phillips and Mrs Hough exchanged amused glances at Winnie's wide-eyed wonder that seemed to leave her speechless. Mrs Phillips leant over and patted her hand. "Don't be afraid," she said, "you'll get used to it." But Winnie was far from afraid. She was shivering with excitement and exultation. This was life. Here she was among the people—millions of them by the look of it—and she, little Nomzamo Winnie Madikizela from those far-off Pondoland hills, was now a part of it. The skyscrapers seemed colossal after the mud huts of the Transkei, and the sight of so many beautiful motor cars made her eyes shine with astonishment.

By the time they reached the hostel most of the inmates had left for work but a handful of students staying there, all of them from urban areas and to Winnie's eyes extremely sophisticated, came to meet this raw new arrival. There were mugs of tea waiting and while Winnie drank hers Mrs Phillips told her how her husband's efforts had resulted in the Hofmeyr School of Social Work being opened in 1943, during the war, to train welfare personnel to serve with the black South African troops in North Africa. When the war ended the school was turned into a college—the only facility of its kind in the country—where blacks could be trained as social workers. It transpired that Winnie was the first rural student to be accepted through a combination of her father's efforts and her own excellent academic record. Mrs Phillips, fearing that Winnie might be steeped in tribal customs and taboos, explained tentatively the religious orientation of both the college and the hostel, but Winnie was able to reassure her at once by describing her own strict religious upbringing.

When the two women left the hostel the day was still young so a group of fellow students took Winnie into town to see some of the splendid shops. She could have gazed in the shop windows for hours, beginning to realize what shoddy wares were sold in the trading stores at home. But her enthusiasm was dampened somewhat by the sight of such poverty in the streets. In the space of an hour she saw several beggars—something she had never encountered before. They were dressed in rags, some deformed or blind, sitting huddled against the shop fronts with hands outstretched for coins from passers-by. All the beggars were blacks.

As the days passed Winnie began to feel the traumatic effect of life in the Big City. She had little realized what a rude awakening it would be to move overnight from an isolated, traditional Pondo home with rural conventions into the hurly burly of bustling, aggressive, apartheid-conscious Johannesburg. Yet in spite of the tremendous contrast to her life in the Transkei she slipped easily into the routine of the Helping Hand Hostel. Being the product of an extended family and having spent years at boarding school, the communal life just suited her. It was the rough and tumble outside the hostel that proved so traumatic after the unhurried way of life in Pondoland. However, the rigid discipline that had been exercised in her home helped her to adapt to the enormous change of environment, despite her initial bewilderment.

She realized how lucky she was to be living in a hostel with its comfortable, conveniently situated accommodation and facilities as well as the companionship she loved. And she was acutely aware of the difference between her own privileged position at a place of higher education and that of the vast majority of black women in Johannesburg. Never did she feel superior, however, only sympathetic. She discovered that life for many black women in that wealthy city centred around a tiny room in an outhouse in the back yard of some palatial white residence where long hours were worked at domestic chores for a pittance plus food and uniforms. For others it was factory work under harsh conditions.

A few of the luckier working girls had accommodation in the hostel and Winnie loved chatting to them and learning about their lives. They were a vociferous crowd of women and seemed to Winnie very knowledgeable. As the weeks passed and she saw for herself how their impoverished lives were in such stark contrast to the opulence of the whites in their beautiful suburbs, she could understand better her father's impassioned teaching about the injustices inflicted on their people. Why, she asked herself, should blacks have so little share of the good things in their own country and so little chance of acquiring them? Why should they be denied the right to live where they pleased, to change their jobs without permission or to enjoy the countless amenities reserved for whites only? She wrote her father long letters describing what she had seen and how furious it made her. In reply Columbus cautioned her that her studies came first and, anyway, political involvement was not for girls.

But it was impossible not to be caught up in the political ferment of the times. All the students at the Hofmeyr School seemed to belong to the African National Congress. Winnie was amazed at their political awareness. While young women at white universities were gossiping about clothes and boyfriends, the black women students spent their tea and lunch breaks discussing the struggle against discrimination and how they could aid it. She also found the working women at the hostel to be well informed and articulate about the political situation. The African National Congress was extremely active and had followers all over the country. Support for the establishment of a black trade union movement was particularly strong. Black trade unions were not legally recognized until 30 years later and then only to a limited degree in order to contain them. In the fifties, however, the workers had no voice and employers were free to exploit the cheap labour that apartheid forced blacks to provide.

Winnie was stimulated by all the political activity, but obedience to her father and her obligation to him made her concentrate on her studies while she remained on the fringe of politics. Determined not to be outdone by all those knowledgeable women, though, she embarked on a course of heavy reading to educate herself about political affairs both in her own and other countries.

When Winnie was accepted at the Hofmeyr School her father was told that he would be required to pay the fees for the first six months. If at the end of that time her progress merited it his daughter would be awarded a scholarship. That alone was a spur to Winnie but it was no hardship to concentrate on her work as she loved her studies. Her lecturers, apprehensive about the experiment to train someone who had never

experienced urban life, were anxious that she should succeed in justifying their insistence that rural students would benefit from advanced
training as much as would their city counterparts. They need not have
worried. Winnie soon outstripped the more worldly city students in
ability, enthusiasm for her work and compassion for those she helped
during her field work projects. Within six months she had done so well
that she was awarded the Martha Washington scholarship, covering
both boarding and tuition fees. This lifted a great load from her father,
who still had several children on his hands.

Columbus had chosen the right vocation for Winnie. Soon she was
recognized as the college's star pupil. She was popular with her fellow
students, too, though they teased her about not having boyfriends. Her
sunny smile and sympathetic nature helped her to make friends and to
keep them, even though her sense of humour sometimes failed to
disguise a streak of bossiness that was to develop over the years into an
autocratic forcefulness of character. Her striking looks did not go
unnoticed either. Reporters and photographers from the black newspapers and magazines often called at the hostel to find suitable subjects
to photograph and frequently they chose Winnie to pose for their
glamour pictures. A few years later she might well have made a great
deal of money from photographic modelling but in those days it was "just
a laugh".

One of the photographers who took pictures of her was Peter
Magubane who was later to suffer repeated arrest and imprisonment
for his politics before eventually leaving to settle in America. In the
meantime he won international recognition for his vivid photographic
portrayals of life in the black townships of South Africa and he went on to
publish several books of his pictures. He and Winnie became firm friends
and years later he joined one of her daughters in the production of a
volume of verse.

It was some while before Winnie had her first sight of Soweto
and when she did it came as something of a shock. The name Soweto
derives from South-Western Townships—there are 26 with more than
a million people living in the sprawling ghetto seventeen miles from
Johannesburg. Winnie had no idea then that it was to become her own
much-loved home.

She went out by bus with some friends. It was dusk and growing dark
when they arrived but there were no street lamps to lighten the way, for
most of Soweto was without electricity. Only now, 30 years later, is work

being carried out to take electricity to the masses there. Smoke from thousands of coal and paraffin fires on which the people cooked threw a pall of grimy cloud over the rows of identical matchbox houses. Some of the townships in Soweto were considerably better than others, but the vast majority of the people lived in squalid surroundings, not by choice, but because they were not allowed to live elsewhere. Inside the houses it was a different story. In the years to come, whenever she entered one of the little dwellings in the course of her work, she was filled with admiration at the attempts, sometimes pathetically inadequate, to create a home in mean surroundings, no matter how poverty-stricken the occupants.

The years of her study slipped by for Winnie with surprising speed. She found Johannesburg more stimulating than she could have imagined. The ANC was on everyone's lips. Protest meetings were being held daily and the success of the ANC's aims was debated endlessly, not everyone agreeing with its passive approach which fell on deaf ears as far as the government was concerned.

The daily newspaper was something Winnie encountered for the first time in Johannesburg. The English language *Rand Daily Mail*, with its sympathetic attitude towards blacks, was a favourite, along with the *Golden City Post*, soon to be banned, and other black papers. Of particular interest to her, in 1955, were reports of the preparations for the forthcoming Congress of the People. This was to be a massive gathering at Kliptown, outside Johannesburg, of representatives of all sections of South African society. It was the first and last of its kind. For months meetings had been organized across the country to collect grievances and appoint delegates to the congress which eventually adopted a document entitled The Freedom Charter as its blueprint for a better South Africa. The Charter called for a democratic state based on the will of the people and asserted that "South Africa belongs to all who live in it, black and white", and included demands that detailed the way this could be brought about.

It was a moderate document by any standards, yet the government saw fit to make it a criminal offence, punishable by imprisonment, to publish copies of it. Winnie thought the Charter magnificent. She has consistently maintained her allegiance to its aims and, even today, readily proclaims: "It is my bible."

Before qualifying for her diploma at the Hofmeyr School, Winnie, along with all the students, had to carry out a course of practical case work in the field. For this she was assigned to the Ncora-Tsolo Rural Welfare Centre in the Transkei. It was run by a Mr Zici, himself a graduate of the Hofmeyr School, and it served a wide, impoverished area of the Transkei, south of Pondoland. Later Winnie was intrigued to realize that the web of fate had sent her to work in the very area from which the black leader, Nelson Mandela, had sprung, though at that time he was still only a legendary figure to her. Tsolo was also the site of Kaiser Matanzima's royal kraal and he, too, was to play a major role in Winnie's life. But that, also, was in the future.

Before taking up her post at Tsolo Winnie travelled to Pondoland to spend a holiday with her father and family. At the end of her stay an unexpected visitor arrived at the homestead. It was the Field Work Director of the School, Professor Hough. He was anxious that his star pupil should do well in her new post so he drove all the way from Johannesburg to take her to Tsolo and see her settled in under Mr Zici. The arrival of a white Afrikaner and his wife in an expensive motor car to transport a young girl from the village was so unheard of that it caused a forest of eyebrows to be raised in the community.

"Aaaaih," bemoaned the elders, shaking their heads in dismay at Columbus, "the poor man has completely lost his daughter." But Winnie and her father were still extremely close and there is no doubt he was immensely proud of his daughter. Not many Pondo girls, he mused, could match Winnie's success. True, she had started out with an advantage, with both parents as teachers, but for much of her life she had been motherless and, apart from books, there had been no trappings of urban civilization in her upbringing. Yet she was coping admirably in the city in competition with those who had grown up there, displaying a self-confidence that was quite remarkable.

At Tsolo Winnie missed Johannesburg dreadfully but her work kept her fully occupied. She had grown up among poor peasants but she had never encountered such poverty as was revealed by her work in this part of the Transkei. The ravages of malnutrition affected an appalling number of children, among whom deaths were common-place, but there was depressingly little she could do to alleviate the suffering.

One day, as she was nearing the end of her stay in Tsolo, she was busy with some paperwork at her desk in the Welfare Centre when an elderly woman from Bizana came in and greeted her.

"Well, my child," said the old crone, unaware of the consternation her words were to cause, "are you pleased about the marriage?"

"What marriage?" Winnie countered, puzzled.

The old woman cackled. "Have they not told you then? They are arranging for you to marry Chief Quaquani's son, the one who is at Lovedale College."

Winnie was shattered. No word of such a plan had reached her. She knew that Chief Quaquani was a member of the same royal house to which Mandela and the Matanzimas belonged, so perhaps her father thought such a marriage would be an advantageous one. But surely not—more likely he was just adhering to the wishes of the tribal elders who arranged these matters. She was aware that traditionally marriage in the tribe was by arrangement, but she had never dreamt that her father would impose the old customs on his emancipated daughter. She had been looking forward with such enthusiasm to returning to the life in Johannesburg that suited her so well and launching out as a fully-fledged social worker. It was unthinkable to give up everything, just on the threshold of her career, to be tied down in marriage to a stranger, possibly becoming one of several wives and being stuck in a remote part of the Transkei for the rest of her life. She had seen too much of the subservience of rural wives and the restricted lives they led even to contemplate such a future for herself. And what of all her years of study? No, it was impossible.

She knew it would be useless to appeal to Columbus not to proceed with the arrangements. Absolute obedience was expected by a father from his children, and she knew, too, that if she stayed in the Transkei, she would be forced into the marriage. There was only one solution— flight. She packed her bags, poured out an explanation to Mr Zici and fled back to the "safety" of the Helping Hand Hostel and the college in Johannesburg.

For a young Pondo woman of nineteen, steeped in the tradition of unquestioning obedience, it was a courageous and daring move and the first time she had ever wilfully gone against her father. It gave her a new-found independence of thought and action she was never to lose.

Back in Johannesburg Winnie wrote at once to her father asking his forgiveness for her flight and explaining that she could not marry yet and would not ever consider an arranged marriage. Her task was made easier as she had some good news for Columbus, too. The examination results were out. She had obtained her diploma in social work with distinction and she had been awarded a prize as the best student. She was all the more thankful to have this good news for Columbus because she had heard from her stepmother how distressed he was about her younger brother, Lungile. Lungile had obtained a phenomenal seven distinctions in the matriculation examination and had been doing brilliantly at Fort Hare University, studying for a B. Sc. degree, when he suffered a mental breakdown from which he was never to recover completely. Winnie hoped that her own success would do something to alleviate her father's sorrow over Lungile's collapse.

Around this time Winnie was invited to a dinner given by Professor Phillips for a group of visiting American professors who had expressed a particular desire to meet the rural student who, they had heard, had managed to adapt so readily to city life and master her sociology studies with such success. She chatted to the American visitors during the dinner but when the evening was drawing to a close they expressed their disappointment to their host that he had been unable to produce the student from an isolated area for their appraisal. Disbelief marked their faces when Professor Phillips told them that the articulate young woman who had spoken to them with such poise was the one they had asked to meet. Their reaction incensed Winnie. She was sufficiently controlled not to show her anger but it shocked her to realize that overseas visitors thought someone from Pondoland would be uncouth. No doubt, she thought, they had expected her to be wearing skins and waving a stick in the streets of Johannesburg.

It was her first introduction to westerners' preconceptions about Africa and it hardened her resolve to challenge that all-too-prevalent ignorance whenever she could.

"As far as I was concerned," she says, "I *was* a raw country girl. I had scarcely been touched by westernization and I still considered myself as completely rural, but to be rural did not mean to be backward and uncouth as they seemed to think."

Though Winnie was the first student from Pondoland at the Jan Hofmeyr School of Social Work, she was also to be one of the last to graduate there. Not long after she left, the School was closed down by the government under the Bantu Education Act. Thereafter, blacks wishing to train as social workers had to do so at what they termed the "bush colleges" in the newly created "homelands". Other than Winnie, probably the best known graduate of the Jan Hofmeyr School is Joshua Nkomo, today leader of Zapu in Zimbabwe. He studied there many years ago as a young student from what was then Southern Rhodesia. Coincidentally, his later rival, Robert Mugabe, Prime Minister of Zimbabwe, was also educated in South Africa—at Fort Hare University.

Chapter Four

SOON AFTER THE announcement of the diploma results Winnie was called to the principal's office. He was smiling broadly as he told her he had some good news. She had been awarded a coveted American scholarship to study for a degree in sociology at a university in the United States. Her fare and all her fees and expenses would be paid.

Winnie was overjoyed at the news. Events were beginning to outstrip her wildest dreams and aspirations. Only that morning she had been wondering how long it would be before she found a suitable post to put her training to good use. Now this award had changed the situation entirely. She rushed out to the post office to send a telegram to her father and stepmother with the news.

Once her studies were over she moved out of the student section of the hostel into the dormitories reserved for working women. There she paid eleven shillings a week for her accommodation, sharing the recreation rooms and communal kitchens where they prepared their own meals. She shared a ten-bed dormitory with a widely differing set of women. The bed right beside hers was occupied by Adelaide Tsukudu, a staff nurse at Baragwaneth Hospital. Adelaide was a Tswana from a completely different area to Winnie—she was brought up on a farm in the Vereeniging district—but the two became firm and lifelong friends and their lives were to be closely linked throughout the years to come in a way that neither could have foreseen.

When Winnie told her friends about the scholarship, conversation in the dormitory included fantasies about life in America, a land none of them had ever envisaged visiting. There was much good-natured envy of the opportunities awaiting their dazzling young friend. Winnie herself combed the library for all the books she could find on America.

Not long after hearing of her award, she was scanning the postboard for letters one day when she was intrigued to find addressed to her an official-looking Baragwaneth Hospital envelope. Baragwaneth is an enormous institution, just on the perimeter of Soweto, and the only hospital in the area for blacks. Winnie's studies had taken her there on

45

many occasions and she had lectured there, too. Nevertheless, she was amazed to find the letter contained the offer of a post at Baragwaneth Hospital as the very first black medical social worker in South Africa.

She caught her breath and sank back on the nearest bench. It was there that Adelaide came across her still sitting staring at the page. Winnie held out the letter for her friend to read. Adelaide, exuberant and demonstrative by nature, gave a shriek of delight and encompassed Winnie in a bearlike hug. Other residents came rushing up to find out what was afoot and the letter was passed from hand to hand.

But now Winnie's dilemma was as great as her jubilation. Quite apart from this being yet another signal honour, it was an offer of the kind of work she had always dreamt of doing. But what of America? As so often happens in life, two wonderful opportunities had come at the same time and she must choose between them. But how could she possibly make such a choice? She veered first one way and then the other, endlessly weighing up the advantages of going to a university abroad and seeing the outside world, against the chance of serving her own people and doing something concrete to help alleviate the appalling social conditions she had come across in Johannesburg over the past three years. She consulted her professor. Though he discussed it with her sympathetically, he was adamant that the choice must be Winnie's alone. Her field work director, Professor Hough, who had helped her so much in her training and encouraged her to work among her own people, was not there to advise her as he had left to further his own studies at the Boston University School of Social Work in the USA, only returning to South Africa in 1957.

Winnie turned to Columbus for advice. His reply, too, was that she must make her own decision yet Winnie felt that between the lines of his carefully phrased letter he was revealing the belief that her own country came first. Winnie thought so, too. At last her mind was made up! She would accept the Baragwaneth post.

When she notified her professor of her decision and her regret at not being able to take advantage of the generous scholarship offered, he told her she could probably take it up at a later date. Subsequent developments denied her that opportunity, but Winnie has never regretted the decision she made that day even though it was to lead, ultimately, to a life of persecution and restriction. It was also the path that led to her later political involvement and fateful meeting with Nelson Mandela.

*

But no presentiment of the miseries ahead clouded Winnie's mind that day in 1956 when she took up her post as South Africa's first black medical social worker. It was a light-hearted, proud, self-assured and happy young woman who faced the press and cameramen while they took photos and wrote stories making much of the achievement of the once barefoot little Pondo girl, imbued with brains, beauty and determination. Winnie sent the cuttings to Columbus.

At Baragwaneth she soon became absorbed in her new job and a favourite with both patients and staff. One of the young doctors at the hospital when Winnie started working there was Dr Nthato Motlana who today, as chairman of Soweto's Committee of Ten, the unofficial mouthpiece of the vast black city, is probably the most influential man in Soweto. At that time he was specializing in paediatrics, having obtained a B. Sc. degree at Fort Hare before qualifying as a doctor at the University of the Witwatersrand Medical School in 1954. Like so many products of Fort Hare in those days, Dr Motlana had joined the Youth League of the African National Congress, later becoming its secretary and, during the Defiance Campaign, like Nelson Mandela and thousands of others, he was arrested and given a nine-month suspended sentence. Immediately afterwards he was banned for five years.

As much of Winnie's work at Baragwaneth was in the paediatric field it was inevitable that she would be in contact with Dr Motlana in the course of her duties. He has a clear memory of those days.

"I met her as a member of staff and right from the start we got on like a house on fire," he recalls. "Working with her was most stimulating and encouraging. She was an outgoing personality, laughing a great deal, very cheerful and intensely concerned about other people's welfare. In hospitals you often find nurses and other staff, even doctors sometimes, who are so impersonal but Winnie was just the opposite. She was a very bright girl indeed and always interested in the problems of others."

At that time there was considerable disaffection among the black doctors at Baragwaneth who were protesting about the intolerable conditions under which they worked. Although they had the same qualifications and did the same work as white doctors on the staff, they received only 60 per cent of the salaries paid to white medical staff. They organized a strike and when this proved ineffectual eighteen doctors resigned. At the end of it all nothing had changed, so Dr Motlana decided to go into the private practice which he has run ever since. He was to become deeply involved in politics and, eventually, a leading figure in Soweto. He and his wife, Sally, kept up their friendship with both Winnie and Nelson (whom Dr Motlana had met at Fort Hare) and remain among their closest friends today. When Nelson was imprisoned he appointed Dr Motlana guardian of his children.

In her work at Baragwaneth Winnie's cheerful, optimistic nature that has been her mainstay through the years enabled her to tackle the dismal situations she encountered. Her field work in Tsolo had introduced her to conditions of extreme poverty in the Transkei, but the urban poverty seemed even more shocking in contrast with the unbelievable opulence of the City of Gold.

When mothers were discharged from Baragwaneth with new-born infants Winnie followed up the cases by visiting them in their homes and was often sick at heart to see the degrading conditions in which many of them were forced to live. Some were in shacks made only of discarded pieces of corrugated iron and cardboard. Rags and newspapers would be stuffed in the cracks to keep out the wind and rain, and stones held down the loose sheets of iron roofing. Malnutrition was rife in the shanty towns, not only because the mothers lacked the means to provide adequate food but also through ignorance of correct feeding. A great many urban babies were illegitimate, the result of casual liaisons between the mothers and migrant workers who usually had a wife in the "homeland", so there was no father to lend support to the new arrival. Often a mother, in despair, would abandon her baby at Baragwaneth.

The first time this happened Winnie consulted a friend, Matthew Nkoane, a senior reporter on a black newspaper, the *Golden City Post*, to see if he could help trace the mother through publicity in the paper. The idea worked and Winnie was able to reunite mother and baby and help them over the first few difficult months. After that initial success she and Matthew worked closely together, tracing not only mothers but relatives of senile patients who had been abandoned at the hospital. And when patients died without any known relatives to claim the body, she enlisted Matthew's help in raising funds through the paper for their funerals. Matthew was later to become a staunch supporter and senior official of the Pan African Congress—the group that was to break away from the ANC. Though the organizations differed on policy, their aims were similar and Matthew and his wife maintained a close friendship with Winnie in spite of their differences.

Winnie stayed on at the hostel in Jeppe. She was extremely happy there and found it enormously stimulating to be in the company of scores of girls from different backgrounds. It was at the hostel that she came into contact for the first time with the black working women of the urban areas. In Pondoland it had been considered undignified for women to leave home to seek work in the towns and those who did so were looked down upon. But in Johannesburg she saw how sheer necessity drove the women to accept menial work in the homes of white people or, if they could find an opening, jobs in the factories, where the wages and conditions were marginally better. Theirs was a hard life. All too often there was no work available and when there was it involved intolerable hours and appalling conditions, all for a pittance. Winnie knew that, given their circumstances, she might have been in the same situation herself. She always lent a sympathetic ear to their problems and listened intently when they discussed their work situations, their efforts to get a living wage; the bus boycotts when fares were raised beyond what they could afford and thousands walked to work rather than pay the increase; and, above all, the iniquities of influx control which determined where a black person should live.

The political situation in South Africa was uppermost in the minds and conversations of the girls. The harsh apartheid measures being introduced by the nationalist government aroused tremendous ill-feeling and resentment. When the girls had sing-songs in the recreation room at night it was always freedom songs they sang, improvising the words and bringing in the names of their revered political leaders.

One of those leaders was Oliver Tambo about whom Winnie had heard a great deal, for he was courting her friend Adelaide. In bed at night, when Winnie would be trying to read, Adelaide would regale her with tales of this clever lawyer who was in partnership with Nelson Mandela and whom she was soon to marry. Not long afterwards Winnie met Oliver. Adelaide had been dressing for a date with him but he arrived before she was ready so when his car pulled up outside she called to Winnie to run down and tell him she would not be long. Winnie gave Oliver the message and stood chatting politely till her friend appeared.

"This is Winnie Madikizela from Bizana," said Adelaide, introducing her friend. Oliver gave a great shout of delighted recognition. "Then you are my niece," he cried. "Welcome, my child, welcome!" Because of the size of Winnie's extended family there were many members whom she had never met. Oliver had remained a stranger, though he had been educated at the Holy Cross Anglican Mission not far from Winnie's home. She was delighted that her friend should be marrying one of her own relatives; already she regarded Adelaide as a sister and now they would really be linked by marriage.

As a hospital Baragwaneth was renowned throughout southern Africa as something of a showpiece. Because of the huge influx of patients, and the variety of wounds and diseases treated there, housemanships at Baragwaneth were much sought-after by newly qualified white as well as black doctors eager to gain the wide experience offered there. One day word spread around the staff that a group of very distinguished people from the Transkei would be making an official visit to the hospital. The VIPs turned out to be Chief Kaiser Matanzima and a retinue of councillors known as Amaphakathi.

Matanzima was favourably regarded by the South African government as he was one of the few leaders in the Transkei prepared to co-operate in their plan to establish ten supposedly independent "Bantu Homelands" in fragments of land around the country. Only 13 per cent of the land area was to be utilized for these homelands, although blacks constituted more than 70 per cent of the population. The idea behind the plan was to maintain the reservoir of cheap migrant labour for the white areas while arbitrarily depriving blacks of their South African citizenship by declaring them nationals of these supposedly independent states. At this time the scheme was still very much in its infancy but Matanzima, because of his collaboration, was accorded special status and every courtesy on his visits to Johannesburg. The vast hospital was spruced up for his arrival and the staff alerted to the importance of the occasion.

Matanzima and his party progressed swiftly through the many sections of the hospital but when they called in at the social welfare department the tour stopped right there. Matanzima was fascinated by Winnie. He questioned her at length about her work at Baragwaneth and eventually suggested that she should join him in the Transkei and run the Ncora-Tsolo welfare centre where she had done her field work. Out of politeness Winnie promised to consider the proposal but she explained that she had not been long at Baragwaneth and was enjoying her work there immensely. Matanzima would not be put off. He said it would be best if they discussed it over a dinner appointment and there and then he arranged with one of his councillors to pick Winnie up after work. Winnie ran along to Adelaide's ward to explain why she would not be accompanying her back to the hostel that evening. Adelaide was intrigued. "He must fancy you, my child," she said.

That evening Matanzima's councillor was waiting in a dilapidated green Oldsmobile to drive her to a corner house in Orlando West, a township of Soweto, where Matanzima was waiting. Winnie saw that he had gone to elaborate lengths to lay on a candlelight dinner for her. "Adelaide was right," thought Winnie. "This is more than just a professional interest."

It was weeks later before Winnie discovered that both the car in which she had been picked up and the house in which Matanzima had entertained her belonged to Nelson Mandela. Nelson, though three years the younger, is Kaiser's uncle. Being so close in age they grew up together so it was a natural, brotherly gesture for Nelson to lend Kaiser his home and his car during his visit.

Matanzima's stay in Johannesburg was a brief one on that occasion but when he returned to the Transkei he bombarded Winnie with several letters each week. It was soon obvious to Adelaide, if not to the inexperienced Winnie, that he intended marriage and her view was confirmed when he confided to her that he hoped to marry Winnie.

When told this, Winnie pooh-poohed the idea, but then came word that Kaiser's councillors were preparing to negotiate with Columbus for his daughter's hand. Winnie was mortified when she heard this. Suddenly she realized how naïve she had been in answering Kaiser's letters, however innocent the tone of her replies. Pointedly she stopped writing; her silence brought Kaiser rushing back to Johannesburg to find out why her letters had dried up. Had Kaiser continued as the only man in Winnie's life it is possible she might have ended up by marrying him, though she remains adamant that she would never have done so as his politics are so opposed to her own. However, the matter was never put to the test, for while Kaiser was still plying her with his interminable romantic letters Winnie had met Nelson Mandela.

Chapter Five

ONE DAY, WHILE Winnie was waiting at a bus stop, her nose buried as usual in a book, a loud hooting drew her attention as Oliver Tambo in his battered blue Ford, with Adelaide as a passenger, stopped alongside.

"Jump in," Adelaide called to Winnie, "we'll give you a lift back to the hostel but we're going to stop for some food first, I'm famished." They pulled in at Adelaide's favourite Greek take-away on a corner of Bree Street in downtown Johannesburg where none other than Nelson Mandela was at the counter being served.

"Buy whatever you want and be sure to get Nelson to pay," laughed Oliver when he spotted Nelson through the shop window. Adelaide was gone so long they thought she must be buying up the whole place. Eventually she emerged with Nelson in tow to introduce him to her friend. "Winnie is also from Bizana," said Oliver, "surely you have seen her pictures in *Bantu World* and *Drum*—she is always dancing about their pages."

Awestruck at meeting Nelson Mandela in person, Winnie remembers little of that first encounter. She maintains she was overcome by shyness, something contrary to her nature but induced here by her early conditioning to behave deferentially towards a tribal chief. Nelson had seemed scarcely to notice Winnie but she must have made an impression, for the very next day he telephoned her at her office at Baragwaneth Hospital to invite her to dinner. It was to be preceded by a consultation, he said, to discuss ways of boosting the Treason Trial Fund.

Like the majority of South Africans, Winnie had been following the progress of the Treason Trial ever since the previous year when police with sten guns had made dramatic dawn swoops all over the country, arresting virtually every prominent member of the ANC from the president, Chief Albert Luthuli, downwards. Nelson and Oliver were both among the 156 now out on bail facing charges of high treason. The Treason Trial Fund had been set up to help pay their crippling legal costs and to give support to the families of those who had lost their jobs when they were arrested.

Nelson told Winnie that, though many generous contributions had come from sympathizers overseas, much more money was going to be needed and he felt she might well have some new ideas about raising it. This seemed an extraordinary suggestion to Winnie as she had never been involved in fund-raising and could not imagine how she would be able to help. She had no thought of demurring, however, and agreed that Sunday would be a suitable time to meet.

The Treason Trial was to drag on for more than four years, at the end of which all were to be acquitted; but when Nelson and Winnie first met the Sword of Damocles was still hanging over his head. Not only was he an awaiting-trial prisoner out on bail but he was a banned person, prohibited from attending or addressing gatherings and severely restricted in his movements. All this made no difference to his confidence. Though forbidden to make speeches his messages went out just the same in his prolific writings. He was thirty-eight, six foot three and broadly built, immaculately dressed and self-assured; a sought-after lawyer and a hero to the people. Yet he was human after all for he was to fall in love with a twenty-year-old girl. From the day he met Winnie she became an obsession and he was determined to marry her.

On the evening of their meeting Nelson did not call for Winnie himself. According to custom, he sent a friend to fetch her on his behalf. This was Joe Matthews, a former Fort Hare colleague and Youth League activist and son of Professor Z. K. Matthews, South Africa's first black professor. Father and son were both treason trialists with Nelson. Joe drove Winnie to Nelson's office where she remembers being petrified as Nelson rose to greet her. He was casually dressed in blazer and flannels. She kept her eyes fixed on the blazer pocket badge of a map of Africa while she waited, tongue-tied. But Nelson soon put her at her ease and within minutes she was laughing with him, completely captivated, she says, by his charisma and his fatherliness, though his feelings for Winnie were not exactly those of a father!

Winnie marvelled at the way he refused to allow the gravity of his own situation to cloud the atmosphere, appearing so confident and optimistic. They discussed the Treason Trial Fund for a while before walking round to a nearby Indian restaurant, called Azad, where Nelson had ordered a curry meal. While they waited to be served he asked Winnie about her life in Pondoland and told her of his own origins, much of which she knew already from reading the many articles written about him. Nelson told her he was a member of the Great House of the Royal Thembu line and therefore superior in status to his nephews, Kaiser and George Matanzima, who were from the lesser or right-hand house. Almost at once Winnie realized that at that point she should mention that she knew Matanzima who had been paying court to her, but the moment passed and Nelson carried on with his tale, blissfully unaware that he had a serious rival in his nephew.

Years later Kaiser and George Matanzima were to become President and Prime Minister respectively of the puppet Transkei state set up by the South African government, their collaboration rewarded with valuable farms and a status higher than that to which they were born. Kaiser was made a paramount chief, creating a precedent in tribal law. His brother, George, was appointed Transkei Minister of Justice before becoming Prime Minister, regardless of the fact that he had been struck off the South African roll of attorneys for misappropriating trust funds and for lying to the Supreme Court. The brothers' political stance was vehemently opposed by Mandela and their cousin, Paramount Chief Sabata Dalindyebo, both of whom regarded so-called independence as a sell-out of the blacks. Subsequently Dalindyebo was heavily fined for insulting the Matanzima brothers (the charge was actually treason) and eventually left the country to join the ANC in exile.

But those developments were in the future. When Nelson told Winnie about his boyhood he explained that as his father had died when he was twelve, he had been brought up with Kaiser, George and Sabata. With the same background and schooling it was all the more remarkable, therefore, that in manhood their politics took them in diametrically opposite directions.

It was at Fort Hare University that Nelson met Oliver and many others who thought the same way politically. Winnie was intrigued to learn that at that time Oliver had been contemplating entering the Anglican ministry. Instead he took a post as mathematics master at St Peter's School in Johannesburg and later turned to law.

Nelson told Winnie that he himself became a lawyer on the urging of Walter Sisulu, who was full of acumen and sound common sense. Walter had had to leave school in Standard Four to support his family; he had worked down the mines, as a "kitchenboy" and in a bakery, all the time studying to improve himself. He had been one of the original members of the Youth League and was now secretary-general of the ANC and one of its most highly regarded members, filled, as they all were, with a burning political zeal. It was Walter, Nelson told Winnie, who had urged him to prepare himself for the struggle by continuing his law studies at the University of the Witwatersrand and becoming articled to a white lawyer in order to qualify as an attorney. The two were firm friends.

In 1952, while Winnie was still at school and the Defiance Campaign was under way, Nelson and Oliver had set up a legal practice known as Mandela and Tambo, the first black lawyers to open offices in the centre of Johannesburg. They had only been able to do that because the offices they rented were in a building still owned by a sympathetic Indian. The government was then in the process of moving all non-whites out of white areas, but several properties in white areas were still Indian-owned. Many attempts had been made to force the new partnership out to the distant black townships far from their clients in jail and the courts, but so far, Nelson revealed, these had been unsuccessful.

He was interrupted in his story by the arrival of the waiter with huge plates of curry. Winnie was dismayed. It was the first time she had tasted Indian food and, accustomed as she was to plain boiled meat, she was unprepared for the shock to her palate. The curry was so hot (or so it seemed that first time) that it made her choke; her nose started running and her eyes watering, not only from the highly spiced food but from mortification at being seen to be such an unsophisticated diner. As he tucked in, Nelson said that he could happily eat curry three times a day. Winnie stored away that piece of information and in the coming months, whenever Nelson introduced her to Indian friends, she persuaded them to show her the way they cooked. It was not long before she became an expert and since then she has been noted for her curries. But on that first occasion it required a real effort to eat most of her helping, and never was she so glad to finish a meal.

Any feeling she may have had that that first date was a fiasco was soon dispelled when Nelson arrived at her office the very next day, ostensibly to discuss some aspect or other of the fund-raising project, though the subject tended to crop up less and less in their animated conversation. The visits became an almost daily occurrence. Much of the time Nelson and Winnie were fencing light-heartedly, like any couple, to discover their true feelings for each other. But their romantic forays went hand-in-hand with more serious matters. Nelson left Winnie in no doubt as to his dedication to the liberation struggle. She was horrified to hear of the many injustices he encountered daily in his legal practice and of the thousands of blacks whom the courts turned into technical criminals for infringement of the petty apartheid laws. She learnt at first hand all about the Treason Trial and the defence they intended to put up.

Winnie was tremendously flattered by Nelson's friendship but mystified, too. Confident as she was in her daily life, she found it hard to convince herself that the great Mandela was interested in her personally. Fearing she may have misread the situation she was reluctant to discuss it with Adelaide, who knew nothing of the assignations with Nelson.

Meanwhile Kaiser Matanzima returned to Johannesburg from the Transkei to find out why Winnie had stopped answering his letters. He phoned her at the hospital to tell her, peremptorily, that she would be picked up after work and driven to the house in Orlando West where he would be having a discussion with some senior chiefs and would see her afterwards. No doubt because of his status he took her consent for granted.

Again Winnie was driven to the same house, still unaware that it was Nelson's home. She knocked on the door which, to her amazement, was opened by two imposing-looking men—Nelson and Kaiser. Simultaneously both men put out their hands in greeting, each trying to work out how Winnie knew the other. They asked her to wait in the dining-room while they finished their consultation in the sitting-room. Both men looked mystified as they left her. Winnie watched them through the open door as they joined several grey-headed men locked in earnest conversation.

She was terrified at the predicament in which she had unwittingly landed herself. How could she possibly deal with both Nelson and Kaiser together? She regarded both men with sufficient awe to address them always with the title "chief". Never had she suspected that the relative's house Kaiser used in Johannesburg actually belonged to Nelson. She blanched to think how her inexperience had led her to become embroiled, however innocently, with both men at the same time.

The more she wondered what they would each say to her, the more panic-stricken she became. To make matters worse, she felt very conspicuous and out of place in her hospital uniform—a white lab coat marked with the words "social worker". There had been no opportunity to go home for a change of clothing when Kaiser's summons had come. What could she do?

While the discussion was going on in the sitting-room she took a quite uncharacteristic step. She simply bolted and dashed back to the sanctuary of her office in Baragwaneth, leaving the two men to work things out for themselves.

Till now Winnie had had no close relationships with men. Her fellow-students always teased her for not having a boyfriend and for not, as they thought, being interested in men, but Winnie had simply had no time for casual romance and, once she met Nelson, no other man existed.

Meanwhile Kaiser and Nelson discovered the other's attraction to Winnie. It led to some acrimonious exchanges between them—now they were rivals in love as well as in politics. Eventually, not without bitterness, Kaiser relinquished his supposed claims upon Winnie, leaving the field clear for his uncle; but once Nelson and Winnie were married Kaiser honoured Winnie's traditional position in the family and to this day refers to her as his aunt, though she is considerably his junior.

Having sorted out the position with his nephew, Nelson resumed his attentions to Winnie, and she could no longer doubt the direction which they were taking. It was a strange romance, for many of their discussions were about the political situation. Nelson, who was president of the Transvaal ANC, explained to Winnie how he and his colleagues were committed to the total abolition of apartheid and oppression of the blacks. This was not a struggle for blacks alone, he said, but for everyone who believed in democracy and equality. That Nelson was just as much at home with people of other races as he was with his own kind was borne out by the fact that his closest confidants were drawn from every racial group in South Africa. It is not race but racism that is the problem, he would tell her, adding that in any event it was a mistake to analyse the situation in terms of colour alone: economics and class were equally important.

Somehow Winnie had managed to keep secret from her friends her assignations with Nelson. Adelaide still believed Winnie might marry Kaiser in spite of Winnie's vehement denials, so she was utterly amazed to discover the truth, casually revealed by Oliver. When Adelaide called at the office one day to collect Oliver there was an exceptionally long queue of clients stretching right out into the street.

"Surely you don't still have to see all those?" she asked incredulously.

"No," laughed Oliver, "those are all Nelson's clients. He will have to deal with them when he can tear himself away from Winnie."

Adelaide was astounded. She could not believe Winnie had kept quiet about such a momentous matter as her growing romance with Nelson. At the hostel she spread the word around and when Winnie walked in she was greeted by a barrage of good-natured banter and laughter as they revealed that all was known. In vain did Winnie protest that things had progressed no further than "going out together". But Nelson persisted with his intentions and on 10 March 1957 he asked Winnie to marry him.

It was to be his second marriage. In his youth he had married a nurse, Edith Ntoko, who had borne him three children, two sons and a daughter. Later they were divorced. Unlike his rural relatives, Nelson did not practise polygamy, so the choice of a wife was particularly important, especially now that he had matured into a person of such stature. Young though Winnie was, he must surely have recognized in her, apart from her obvious physical attractions, those sterling attributes that were to make her the perfect wife for him. His only doubt was whether he had the right to ask her to share his uncertain life.

His proposal to Winnie was made during a picnic on a white-owned farm along the Evaton Road, south-west of Johannesburg. There he told her of the depth of his feelings for her but added that he must point out all the disadvantages of their relationship: he was awaiting trial and could go to prison for a long time; he was being hounded continually by the police and no doubt she would be, too, if she married him; and, most important of all, he had dedicated his life to his people's fight against discrimination, injustice and apartheid and that fight must take precedence over everything, even his personal feelings. "It is a commitment for life, like a call to the ministry," he told her.

He described to Winnie the part he was playing in trying to organize the people in both town and country. He had drafted a scheme called the M Plan to organize ANC volunteers on a street basis, so there would always be someone in touch with the people to keep them informed and draw them into the struggle. With Walter, Oliver and others, he was now spearheading the struggle against the government but it was a dangerous path they were treading and he wanted her to have no illusions about that.

Winnie was captivated both by the man and his dream. The chance to help Nelson realize that dream was the opportunity for which she had been searching since those days at home in Pondoland, when she had listened with such youthful indignation to the tales of all the wrongs suffered by blacks in South Africa over generations past. She knew she could identify completely with Nelson's ideas, and when she pledged her love she pledged, too, her own dedication to the cause. From that day

Nelson's hopes and plans became hers. She was utterly committed, with a strength of purpose from which nothing has been able to shake her through a quarter of a century of harassment.

As the Treason Trial progressed, the cases against many of the 156 accused were withdrawn until only 30, including Nelson, remained to face the charges. He and Winnie knew that if he were found guilty even the death penalty was a possibility. Nevertheless, they decided to go ahead with their intention to marry—knowing full well that if they were to carry out their commitment to their people their chances of leading a normal life were minimal.

Custom decreed that Winnie's father had to be approached for his consent to the marriage. Nelson was unable to travel to Pondoland to see Columbus in person because he was prevented by his banning order from leaving the magisterial district of Johannesburg, so he sent Winnie herself to inform her father of their intention to marry. And he asked his nephew, George Matanzima, to negotiate the lobola for Winnie. Years later, when George was found to have misused trust funds, one of Winnie's relatives caused considerable amusement by remarking wryly that had this wayward tendency surfaced earlier the lobola might well have been at risk.

Lobola is the name given to the bride price, traditionally paid with cattle by the bridegroom to the bride's father. This is one reason why daughters are so highly prized! About ten head of cattle are average, but if the bride is from a well-placed family or has special attributes considerably more cattle are handed over. In any event it is always a matter for bargaining—a long-drawn-out preliminary to every marriage and a process everyone enjoys.

When Winnie broke the news to her father he was aghast. He said he could not imagine anyone wanting to marry a man awaiting trial from whom she might be separated for ever—especially after she had turned down not one, but two, advantageous offers of marriage. However in this case Hilda, Winnie's stepmother, with whom she had such an affectionate relationship, took a hand in persuading Columbus to approve Winnie's choice. Though he shook his head in dismay, Columbus, knowing of old that Winnie had a will of iron and could prove intractable, buried his doubts and gave in.

There was a great deal of excitement at the homestead when George Matanzima arrived from the royal kraal to negotiate the lobola. After several days of bargaining agreement was reached but, as the bride is never told how many cattle she is worth, Winnie does not know to this day how many beasts Nelson pledged for his wife.

The tribal elders impressed upon Columbus how important it was to plan the wedding in keeping with the status of the bridegroom who was not only a member of the Great House of the Thembu but a beloved figure to many millions. Columbus and Hilda discussed the preparations at length while Winnie was back at her work at Baragwaneth Hospital. Eventually it was decided that in deference to all the city dwellers who would be travelling long distances to attend, there would be a formal, western-style reception in the village of Bizana before the traditional celebrations at home in the hills, where the whole district of many hundreds of people would turn out as a matter of course.

The only possible venue for a big formal wedding reception was the Bizana Town Hall which was an exclusive white preserve. No blacks had ever been allowed to use it but Columbus took the plunge and applied to hire it. To everyone's amazement the request was granted, presumably on instructions from a government suddenly anxious to appear well-disposed towards those whom it planned to involve in the scheme for an "independent" Transkei. Whatever the reason for this rare turn-about in apartheid policy, no obstacles were placed in the way of the preparations.

With a lawyer for a bridegroom due attention was paid to the legal aspects of the marriage for which an ante-nuptial contract was drawn up. Winnie was one of the few black women of her generation to take advantage of that facility which gives a woman control over her possessions. Without such a contract, marriage in South Africa is automatically in community of property which gives the husband extensive powers over his wife. It always angers Winnie that black women are permanent minors in South Africa. "A black woman," she says "faces a three-fold disability in this country: she has to overcome the disadvantage of being black, the disadvantage of being a woman and the disadvantage of her African cultural background in an essentially westernized environment."

By the time the wedding date drew near Winnie had been introduced to a great many of Nelson's friends and was taking a keen interest in the work and operations of the ANC. It was obvious to their friends that Nelson was grooming her to play an important role in the movement and that she was well fitted for that. She was not yet regarded as a threat by the authorities, though Nelson, out on bail while the Treason Trial dragged on, was under constant surveillance as a banned person. He had to make special application to attend his own wedding and was granted leave to absent himself from Johannesburg for just four days.

Meanwhile, in Pondoland the even tenor of rural life had been disturbed by all the preparations for the wedding—the most important event to occur in the district for many years. An air of excitement pervaded the homestead—even extending to the homes of relatives farther afield—and there was much arguing about which cattle were to be slaughtered to feed the expected huge crowd.

While the men busied themselves with such considerations the women made vast quantities of beer—the traditional weak brew with the consistency of gruel, made from sorghum or mealies. They stamped maize and prepared dishes to accompany the meat which would be cooked in huge iron pots. Guests at a wedding feast were entertained lavishly as a matter of course.

Nelson and Winnie were married in the Methodist Church in Bizana on 14 June 1958. Winnie wore a white satin and lace bridal gown and veil for the ceremony. At the town-hall reception that followed there were lengthy formal speeches, with Columbus taking full advantage of his captive audience to lecture the city guests—warning them to clear the mists from their eyes and realize what was happening in their country. Eventually the guests piled into cars and buses to drive to eMbongweni for the traditional uninhibited merry-making to which they had all been looking forward. Many stayed on for a full week of feasting and dancing. One face absent from the guests was that of Winnie's great friend, Adelaide, now married to Oliver Tambo. She was about to give birth and was unable to make the long journey to the Transkei, though her husband, both as Nelson's partner and close colleague in the ANC, as well as a relative of the Madikizelas, was one of the special guests.

At the end of those four days Nelson and Winnie waved goodbye to their guests and set off back to Johannesburg. They took with them the wedding cake which, according to tradition, should be cut at the bridegroom's homestead in front of the family elders. There has been no opportunity to carry out this custom, so Winnie has the cake still, waiting for Nelson's release. Miraculously, and perhaps symbolically, the cake has never crumbled away.

Chapter Six

THE NEWLY WED couple returned to Johannesburg full of optimism, even though the indications were that their time together would be short-lived. Nevertheless, they were determined to live normally and to start a family while they had the chance. Winnie made up her mind not to let fear sully their happiness. "I was very young and naïve then, but Nelson was wonderfully supportive and he had a marvellous way of imparting his own strength and courage to others," she says.

Nelson took his bride to the Soweto township of Orlando West to the corner house which the Johannesburg municipality, many years previously, had allocated to him for life on a rental basis. It is No 8115 (houses in the townships are known by numbers and not by street names), an address imprinted on the minds of many security policemen who have, over the years, spent countless hours watching it and raiding it in the unfulfilled hope of catching the occupants in the act of doing something illegal.

The Mandela house, though modest by white South African standards, was considerably better than the majority of the matchbox dwellings in Soweto. It even had the quite exceptional (for Soweto) luxuries of electricity, hot water and an indoor bathroom. Though Winnie had visited Soweto hundreds of times in the course of her work and to see friends this was the first time she had lived there, the Helping Hand Hostel having been her home until her marriage.

She settled in happily to her new life—all her spare time being devoted to helping Nelson in his work for the ANC. The house was always full of people and laughter and Winnie found the constant comings and goings, the discussions and arguments, stimulating and encouraging. Encouragement she needed to face the tension of Nelson's protracted trial, which was to strain even her indomitable spirit.

One night, soon after their marriage, Winnie and Nelson were asleep when there was a sudden violent banging on the front door of their house.

"For a few moments I thought that a tornado had struck," recalls Winnie. "It was one thirty-five in the morning and I was convinced something terrible must have happened but Nelson, who was wide awake and out of bed in an instant, told me not to be alarmed—it was only a police raid. They were banging with their truncheons, flashing bright torches through the windows, shouting at us to open up and making enough noise to waken the whole neighbourhood."

Winnie knew that Nelson's home and offices had been raided frequently, but she had not realized the reality would be so alarming and distasteful.

"There were these coarse Boer policemen thumbing through our personal belongings, pulling books off shelves, turning drawers of clothing upside down, reading our letters, rough handling our possessions and all the time passing derogatory and derisory remarks about kaffirs. It was horrible. And it was all for nothing. They couldn't find anything incriminating. After they had gone we tidied up the mess and I made coffee before we went back to bed. Nelson warned me I would have to get used to raids like that, but afterwards they never seemed quite so traumatic as that first time, though the attitude of the security policemen who carry out the raids always makes my blood boil. They are so uncouth."

Soon after Winnie's marriage Dr Hendrik Verwoerd, the ruthless Minister of Native Affairs, described by Chief Albert Luthuli as "the most ardent and relentless apostle of apartheid", became Prime Minister of South Africa. His accession was to spur on opponents of the system to greater protests. There were demands for a £1 a day minimum wage for their work, abolition of the Group Areas Act, the vicious permit system, the increase in the poll tax and, above all, an end to the scheme to extend to women the hated pass laws that hitherto had applied only to men. Now the government intended to make it mandatory for all black women to carry passes at all times, just as men had to do.

Passes are identity documents called reference books bearing a photo and particulars of the holder. A pass must be carried at all times by blacks over the age of sixteen. It is no excuse to mislay a pass or leave it at home, and loss of a pass can turn a normally law-abiding person into one with a criminal record. Passes regulate the movement, the employment, the place of abode and the family life of millions of blacks. They have been the means of uprooting whole communities and separating husbands and wives when the pass of one does not permit residence in the same area as the pass of the spouse. They number among the most widely loathed of all the discriminatory laws.

South Africa has, proportionately, one of the highest jail populations in the world. Every year nearly half a million people are imprisoned for pass offences alone. These technical offenders find themselves flung into prison in the same way as robbers, rapists and murderers. "As a result," says Winnie "it has become part and parcel of city life for a black to be in and out of jail. No longer is there any stigma attached to it. In fact the opposite applies. A family in which no member has ever been imprisoned is highly suspect—they must surely have come to some arrangement with the police to report others in exchange for immunity!" For years Winnie refused to apply for a pass and only did so eventually when told she would not be allowed to visit Nelson without one.

It is a common saying in South Africa that when you cross the (black) women you have struck a rock, and certainly black women in South Africa have been fearless in the fight for their rights. They have endured incredible hardship and brutality in prison, often in solitary confinement, and have been frequently tortured, while women political prisoners have had no study rights and received no remission of sentence. In spite of this they were not slow to come forward in their thousands to support an anti-pass protest in Johannesburg, organized by the ANC in October 1958, four months after Winnie's marriage. As Nelson's wife and already a prominent member of the Women's League of the ANC, she was in the forefront of the protesters. Winnie is a fierce contender for the liberation of women though not, she emphasizes, a women's libber in the western sense of the word and she was now deeply committed to a path of political involvement.

As the women gathered to make their peaceful but loud protest 1,200 of them, many with babies on their backs, were arrested, pushed into police vans and driven to the Johannesburg Fort. One of the women arrested was Winnie. It was her very first taste of prison and of the vicious treatment that was to be her lot. The women were crammed into foul-smelling cells in which there was barely room for them to lie down on the cement floors. Each was given one filthy blanket smelling of urine and the place was riddled with lice. Winnie, pregnant with her first child, was revolted at the dirt and the smell.

The shock of her arrest, the jolting and shoving and the horrendous prison conditions caused her to start haemorrhaging. She knelt on the cold stone floor, her head in her hands, while all around her babies were crying and women pushing and struggling to find a corner for themselves in the crush. Winnie was distraught. Was she to lose the child that they both wanted so much? Just then a comforting voice asked her, "What is it, my child?" It was Albertina Sisulu, Walter's wife and a trained midwife. Winnie had never been so glad to see anyone, and as soon as she had explained the situation Albertina took charge. She would brook no interference, shoving women out of the way to make room for Winnie to stretch out flat. Then she wrapped her in her own overcoat to keep her warm on the cold prison floor, prevented her from moving and per-suaded her to eat some of the revolting prison food when it was brought to the cell. Thanks to Albertina's ministrations, Winnie's threatened miscarriage was averted and the child saved, even though Winnie was to spend a nightmarish fortnight in jail before she was released.

When she came out of prison the joy of her reunion with Nelson was overshadowed by the news that she had been sacked from her post at Baragwaneth Hospital for taking part in the pass protest. It was a bitter blow. Winnie loved her work and took tremendous pride in doing it well and showing an interest in the people she helped. The money from her salary was very necessary, too. Since Nelson could attend to his practice only on a part-time basis in between court appearances, his earnings were reduced to a pittance.

Winnie's dismissal provoked a storm of protest. Friends notified the press about it and the papers carried reports of how the star pupil of the Jan Hofmeyr School of Social Work and South Africa's first black medical social worker, having forgone an American scholarship to serve her own people, had been dismissed ignominiously for championing the rights of women. Those reports had no effect on the authorities who had ordered her dismissal but, to Winnie's great joy and relief, they brought her the offer of a job as a social worker with the prestigious Johannes-burg Child Welfare Society. It was a post she was to hold with distinction for the next four years.

Many years later Winnie was to be given the accolade "Mother of the Nation", but even in the days of her youth her compassionate nature inspired affection among the case families she visited to help. Soon it was not just as Nelson Mandela's wife, but as a person in her own right, that she gained widespread regard throughout Soweto.

When Nelson and Winnie married, their mutual friend, Dr Nthato Motlana, became the family doctor. It was he who attended Winnie when their first child was born in 1959. In spite of the threatened miscarriage in the early months of pregnancy Winnie had suffered no ill effects and, though now heavily pregnant, she was in her usual good spirits when Nelson left to attend an out-of-town executive meeting of the ANC that would keep him away for a while. But, he assured Winnie, he would be back in good time for the birth. He was not.

Winnie's labour pains began before he returned. There was no shortage of relatives and friends to see her safely to Baragwaneth Hospital for the confinement, but they were not her husband and Winnie, understandably, was peeved. When Nelson reached home the next day and learnt of the birth of a daughter he knew his wife would have been upset at his absence. Winnie's sister gave her an amusing account of how Nelson, in unaccustomed panic, tried to think of ways to excuse his belated return. In the end he decided the only way was to rope in a friend, Duma Nokwe (later to become ANC general secretary until his death), to accompany him to the hospital on his first visit.

"He came tripping in looking very shamefaced and with Duma in tow. It was obvious to me why—he knew I would never upbraid him in front of another," laughs Winnie. Whether she ever did indulge in remonstrance is uncertain. It is difficult to imagine anyone of such forceful character as Winnie playing the submissive wife, yet it is clear she has always idolized Nelson. She maintains that her veneration for him has always been so great that even today she has to check herself in his presence not to call him Madiba Mhlekazi (chief)—which is how she has always thought of him since their first meeting.

The birth had been an easy one and Winnie was delighted with her daughter though a little put out that she would have no say in the naming of the child. That was the prerogative of Chief Mdingi who called the little girl Zenani, meaning "What have you brought?", a name that Winnie abbreviated to Zeni. Zeni was a beautiful child who was to grow up to marry a prince in true fairy-tale style. But first there were to be many years of heart-break partings as her mother sought to protect her from the backlash of venom aimed at her parents.

When Winnie was up and about again more and more of her time was taken up with helping Nelson in his work for the ANC. He was anxious that she should understand all the implications and know his wishes should he not be there to state them himself. With the situation looking graver by the day he decided that Winnie must learn to drive, both because she needed to use a car for her Child Welfare work as well as for

ANC business, and because he realized he might well not be free to drive her around once his trial was over.

Like many an unwitting husband before him Nelson made the cardinal error of deciding that he himself was the best person to teach his young wife to drive. He soon discovered his mistake. Within minutes of the start of the first lesson they were shouting at each other. Normally an even-tempered man, Nelson lost patience with Winnie, telling her she was stupid, uncoordinated and irrational. Teaching her was an impossible task—she would never learn, he said. So saying he stalked off in anger, leaving Winnie sitting in the car on the vacant ground to which he had taken her for her lesson. She was furious, and had to ask three township dwellers who had been watching with amusement to push the car home for her. Nelson's anger was short-lived. Repenting his hastiness he went round to his friend, Joe Matthews, and asked him to take over and teach Winnie to drive, something he readily undertook to do. But that move, too, was destined to fail, though for a different reason.

Tensions that had been developing in the ANC for a number of years were now coming to a head. Some of the members of the Youth League, of which Nelson was president, were critical of what they claimed were the ANC's moderate and ineffectual policies. In particular they were fiercely opposed to any alliance with whites and communists. Often Nelson would stay up late into the night arguing with dissidents in a vain attempt to heal the rift that was developing within the organization. Winnie recalls how he would crawl into bed in the early hours, clearly exhausted but burning with rage. He would ask her how they could speak of wanting a free country when all they really wanted was to replace one form of racism with another. Surely, he would ask, they could see that the struggle hinged on making people of all races learn to live together without tearing the country apart in the process.

Time and again he would warn Winnie to beware of opportunists. They wanted excitement and high drama but they shied away from doing the donkey work of organizing the people. "I am afraid they are going to make trouble," he said.

Nelson's words were prophetic. In April 1959, a militantly nationalist group broke away from the ANC and, under the leadership of Robert Sobukwe, formed the then rival Pan Africanist Congress. Sobukwe, at that time a young man, and six years Nelson's junior, was a university lecturer who had studied at Fort Hare. Significantly, many leaders of consequence throughout the African continent were once students at Fort Hare. As well as Nelson, Oliver, Sobukwe and Mugabe, Chief Gatsha Buthelezi, Chief Minister of Zululand, and many others studied there. Through his involvement in the ANC Nelson had come to know Sobukwe well and the two, though differing on many issues, shared a mutual respect.

The pass laws were still a burning issue throughout the country. The ANC was planning a national anti-pass campaign to begin on 31 March 1960, the anniversary of the pass burnings that had taken place as long ago as 1919. Increasingly, the house at 8115 Orlando West resembled a campaign headquarters more than a quiet domestic abode. Winnie revelled in all the activity and began to show, for the first time, the organizational ability and leadership qualities that were to distinguish her in the years ahead.

At the beginning of March all the ANC plans took a knock when the PAC, in an attempt to pre-empt the ANC initiative, announced its own pass-law resistance campaign scheduled for 21 March, ten days earlier than the ANC's planned protest. Nelson knew it was folly for the PAC to rely on mass spontaneity as a substitute for sound organization such as the ANC was carrying out, but he and Winnie were watching developments closely to see how the PAC plan would fare.

On 21 March Winnie stayed at home listening to the news broadcasts and gathering information wherever she could. News came that Sobukwe had been arrested but at first it seemed that, other than in Cape Town, only a handful of supporters in the big cities had responded to his call. It appeared that everything was fizzling out. Then in mid-afternoon Beatrice, one of Winnie's co-workers in the Women's League of the ANC, burst through Winnie's front door, breathless and almost incoherent. Beatrice lived in Vereeniging, 50 miles south of Johannesburg.

"Haaai Winnie!" she gasped. "The police are shooting them everywhere." Beatrice was a big woman, well over forty, and her large frame coped ill with her agitated state. She was shaking all over and perspiration was running down her face, mingling with her tears. Alarmed, Winnie pressed her into a chair and made her drink a glass of water. Beatrice's agitation had transferred itself to Winnie. "I don't know what the hell you are saying. Try to tell me slowly."

Beatrice wiped her face and began again, her expression lending more horror to her story than her tears had done. She told how she had been packing groceries into her car that morning when she had heard of big crowds gathering in Sharpeville, a dormitory township outside Vereeniging, and had decided to drive out there to see what was going on. She had watched and waited for hours, talking with some of the crowd of about 5,000 who were gathered peacefully outside the police station. The air force had swooped low overhead several times during the course of the morning and then, just before lunch, a large contingent of extra police had arrived in armoured cars. But no one was concerned. Someone at the back of the crowd told Beatrice the people were waiting for an important announcement that was going to be made about the pass laws.

"The people were laughing and chatting. It was like a holiday. Then suddenly I heard these shots, shots, shots, shots. Everyone was screaming and pushing madly to get away but the police kept firing. There were dead people lying on the ground everywhere. I couldn't look any more. I rushed to my car and drove like a mad woman to tell you what has happened," said Beatrice.

Winnie was aghast at her story which spread rapidly throughout Soweto, but it was only later that the full extent of the massacre became known: 69 killed outright, including eight women and ten little children—most of them shot in the back—and nearly 200 others with gunshot wounds.

Meanwhile unrest had spread to the black townships of Langa and Nyanga in Cape Town. In the ensuing week the streets of Cape Town were alive with demonstrators angrily protesting. Thousands of blacks stayed at home to protest. When they congregated in Langa the police opened fire. Altogether fourteen were killed and scores wounded during the Langa unrest.

Although the shootings at Sharpeville and Langa were by no means the first shootings of blacks by the white police force, never before had the brutality of the regime received such widespread international publicity. The effect on the economy was almost disastrous. In one day alone the market capitalization of the Johannesburg Stock Exchange dropped £70 million and for the first quarter of 1960 it dropped by £600 million. Had it not been for the enormous financial backing South Africa received from overseas its recovery would have been doubtful.

Differences between the ANC and the PAC were put aside as the ANC President, Chief Albert Luthuli, called for a day of mourning with a nationwide workers' stay-at-home. Leaders of the ANC, anticipating that the ugliness of the situation was bound to result in vicious clampdowns by the government, decided with great foresight to send a representative abroad where he could operate without restriction.

Nelson's law partner, Oliver Tambo, was selected. Hasty preparations were made so that he could leave before the anticipated arrests began. Just a week after Sharpeville, on 27 March, Oliver said goodbye to his family and close associates and was driven by a friend, Ronald Segal, to Botswana. They had intended going on to what was then Southern Rhodesia until they were told there was a warrant out for their arrest there. So instead they flew from Gaborone to Nyasaland (now Malawi), only to learn from sympathizers that there was an extradition order out for them in that country. So it was on to Kenya, Tanganyika, Ghana and, finally, London. Oliver Tambo's direction of the ANC from abroad has continued to the present day. He is now based in Lusaka, the capital of Zambia, where the ANC has its headquarters.

Back in South Africa the ANC protest strike had been seen by the ANC as a huge success and by the government as a failure. In some parts there was a 90 per cent response but in others many went to work as usual. In spite of the ANC's insistence on peaceful behaviour feelings were running so high among the people that the protests turned to unrest with stoning and burning of buildings and passes.

Two days later, as anticipated by the ANC, the government acted. It declared a state of emergency, outlawed both the ANC and the PAC and arrested nearly 2,000 people across the country. Among those detained were Nelson and Chief Luthuli. When Chief Luthuli was eventually released months later it was to the news that he had been awarded the Nobel Peace Prize. After his return from Oslo, where he received the award, he was banished to a remote part of Zululand. There he was later killed, claimed by the government to have been struck by a train as he walked along a railway line.

In Johannesburg Adelaide Tambo was assessing with Winnie and other ANC officials the safest way for her to join Oliver abroad with their two children, Tembi and eighteen-month-old Dali. Three months after her husband's departure she crossed the Swaziland border on foot with her two toddlers. She was disguised as a peasant woman on her way to visit her husband. In the event she was not suspected at the South African border but, for her, the worst ordeal lay ahead. The plans were for her to fly to Ghana and thence to London. She had never been in an aeroplane before nor had she set foot outside South Africa. In addition she no longer had numerous family members around to help care for the two children. She was anxious about the situation at home and deeply worried about her husband abroad and how they would all manage in a strange new country.

For nearly a month she was marooned in Swaziland. That tiny land-locked kingdom is completely surrounded by South Africa and Mozambique, then a Portuguese colony with close ties with South Africa. Eventually arrangements were made for Adelaide and her children to fly to Botswana (then the Bechuanaland Protectorate). Ghana's Kwame Nkrumah sent a plane to fetch her, but the journey's travails were still far from over. The plane had to put down to refuel in Katanga. This was the time (1960) when the former Belgian Congo (now Zaire) was in turmoil. Independence had been hurriedly imposed at the end of June and when the Belgians left the whole country was plunged into a state of virtual anarchy. It was in the midst of this chaos that Adelaide's plane landed in Katanga. She was immediately arrested and jailed overnight but high-level representations secured her release. When she arrived in Ghana it was to discover that she had just missed Oliver who had had to go on to London, though her disappointment was mitigated by the wonderful hospitality she received from Dr Nkrumah.

From Ghana she flew off on the final leg of her journey. At long last, three months after leaving South Africa, her travelling ordeal was over. She arrived in Britian homeless, penniless and separated from the accustomed support of family and friends.

Her husband was directing all his energies to organizing and running the external wing of the ANC so the task of re-establishing a home and providing an income for the family fell squarely on Adelaide's shoulders. Slowly things came right for the Tambos. Adelaide, a qualified nursing sister, had no difficulty in obtaining a Health Service post in London. Oliver was soon joined by many of his trusted lieutenants who had fled South Africa to escape the dragnet. A third child was born to the Tambos in London and their three offspring were brought up as typical English children. Twenty years later their elder daughter was married in St Paul's Cathedral in London, while the other two children are now at universities in France.

Adelaide's concern for Winnie and Nelson has never abated. She, probably more than anyone else, having been brought up on an Afrikaner farm, realizes what banishment to a desolate platteland town must mean to her friend. Winnie, in turn, knows that she can always count on Adelaide. The friendship forged when they slept in adjoining beds in a communal dormitory in their youth and prepared their food together in the hostel kitchen has survived through 24 years of parting. The two have kept in contact, usually by telephone, still regarding each other as sisters.

By this time Winnie's position as branch chairman of both the ANC and the ANC Women's League had nominally disappeared now that the ANC had been banned. But far from curbing her activities the banning meant even more work and more astute planning to keep in touch with the rank and file of the people now that so many leaders were imprisoned.

Among those detained was Joe Matthews whom Nelson had persuaded to take on the task of teaching Winnie to drive. They had had only two lessons before the plan was cut short by his imprisonment. Now Winnie was stranded without transport. She had Nelson's car but no one to drive it, for Nelson's other close associates were locked up with him. Desperation prompted her to teach herself to drive. To begin with she placed broomsticks on the ground to mark a path from the house to the road to practise reversing. She bashed down the garage door in the process, much to Nelson's disgust when he saw it on his release. Winnie, undeterred by her lack of experience, decided that the only way to become proficient was to face the traffic at the wheel of the car but in spite of her self-confidence she realized she needed someone to accompany her to point out the hazards.

At this time Nelson's secretary at his legal practice was a young woman named Ruth Mompati, later to become chief representative of the ANC in London and now based in Lusaka. She and Winnie were great friends so when Winnie offered to drive Ruth to work the offer was accepted gratefully. Her pleasure at this arrangement was short-lived. She had no idea that Winnie was not yet a competent driver. Within minutes of setting off a petrified Ruth was clinging to the car seat in horror as they experienced one hair-raising escape after another on Johannesburg's busy roads—their violent stops and starts punctuated by furious hooting from other motorists. It was Winnie's first venture into the thick of the traffic and Ruth vowed she would never accompany her again. She reckoned without Winnie's persuasive powers. In the days to come Ruth was enticed back into the passenger seat of the car—warning Winnie of approaching hazards and exhorting her to be careful.

Gradually there was an improvement and when Winnie felt she had achieved a sufficient degree of proficiency she made an appointment to take her driving test. One problem remained, however. It was necessary to be accompanied to the testing ground by a licensed driver. Nelson and his colleagues were still in detention and their other friends who could drive were all away at work all day, so there was no one suitable available. But the ever-resourceful Winnie did not allow such a minor matter to deter her. She pulled in to a petrol station near the testing ground and asked one of the attendants to accompany her by pretending to be her driving instructor. He thought it a huge joke and readily agreed.

Winnie passed her driving test at the first attempt—much to Nelson's astonishment when he heard. She has been driving ever since. The car in which she taught herself to drive gave her good service until three years later when it was blown up by a bomb planted by "someone unknown", according to police records. But in Winnie's mind it was just another act of official vandalism designed to intimidate her.

Chapter Seven

THE UPHEAVALS OF 1960 were not confined to the urban areas. Winnie's native Pondoland was the scene of a major revolt.

Though the arrest of Nelson and his colleagues almost overshadowed the disturbing news from home, the situation in Pondoland was never far from Winnie's thoughts and served only to add to her anxieties about events in Johannesburg. For months stories had been filtering through of unrest in the Bizana, Flagstaff and Lusikisiki districts of Pondoland. Relatives who came to visit Winnie would bring her first-hand reports from the troubled areas. Practically nothing appeared in the papers about the situation as the government had clamped down on news from the area.

According to Winnie trouble began when the government introduced what they called the Bantu Authority to replace the Bunga. The Bantu Authority was regarded with deep suspicion by the Pondo tribesmen and when the government amended the Land Trust Act, allowing it to apportion land, cull cattle and zone and fence the various areas of Pondoland, there was widespread resentment. The government claimed it was taking these steps in the interests of land conservation. The Pondos, however, were convinced that the efforts to move them off the lands they had farmed for centuries were merely further moves to force them to seek work on white farms and to provide cheap labour for the mines. Why, they argued, should they be limited in the numbers of cattle they were allowed to keep while white farmers could have vast herds. And if the government was so concerned about conservation why was it forcibly re-settling more and more people in an already overcrowded area, thus exacerbating the already serious soil erosion?

To impose its will the Bantu Authority offered to pay the tribal chiefs to carry out the new scheme. But they reckoned without the wrath of the Pondo tribesmen who organized themselves into groups to form a body called Intaba, which means mountain, to oppose the, Bantu Authority.

74

"The scheme the government wanted to introduce meant the division of grazing lands, the drawing of lines between cornfields and the erection of fences even across graves in the sacred family cemeteries," says Winnie. "I knew how inconceivable such moves would appear to the Pondo tribesmen, steeped in family traditions."

Intaba set out to persuade or coerce the chiefs into rejecting the government scheme. Any chief or headman who refused persistently, was given a final warning and then killed. Twenty of those who preferred to accept government money rather than honour the wishes of the people died in the unrest during which their kraals were burnt. Intaba itself took on the allocation of the communal lands and the Bantu Authority found its proposed scheme disrupted at every turn.

Few in the cities were aware of the seriousness of the situation because of the dearth of reports from the area, but Winnie, knowing the mood of the people, was increasingly apprehensive about events there. She was deeply worried about her family's possible involvement, since her child-hood home was at the heart of the dispute. She knew how fiercely the land reclamation scheme was opposed by the tribesmen and how ruthless the Bantu Authority would be in suppressing its opponents.

Never for one moment did it enter her head that her own father would be considered a collaborator. But she knew the news was bad when Jeremiah, the young migrant worker who had accompanied her on her first journey to Johannesburg in 1953, arrived at her home one day in mid-1960 looking grave and disturbed.

Jeremiah made a point of calling on Winnie each time he returned to Johannesburg from Bizana, bringing her gossip and messages from home. Usually he was jaunty and high spirited but this time she noticed a difference in his approach. They greeted each other in traditional manner and spoke of inconsequential matters at first while Winnie longed to shout: "Get on with it, tell me what has happened." But she restrained herself and, the formalities over, Jeremiah came to the point. The Pondo revolt, he told Winnie, had really come to a head. Intaba had met at Ngquza Hill near the village of Bizana where they had made the decision to take up arms to fight the government on the Land Trust system. However, the authorities learnt of the threatened uprising and rushed a huge, heavily armed force of police, aided by helicopters, to the area to confront the Pondos.

When the assembling tribesmen saw this vastly superior force they came out carrying a white flag and without offering any violence. But,

Jeremiah told Winnie, the police opened fire with machine guns, shooting the surrendering tribesmen in the back as they turned and fled. At least 30 were killed. (According to Winnie later, official statements wrongly gave the number killed as only six and the government tried to play down the Pondo Revolt as a tribal fight, whereas it was the most significant event to have occurred in Pondoland in modern times.) Now Jeremiah paused in his tale and Winnie sensed that he had difficulty knowing how to proceed.

"Your father was involved," he said at last. At that time Columbus was still teaching but he had started the first ever bus service in the district. Jeremiah told Winnie that when the uprising was being planned a number of tribesmen approached Columbus with a request that he use his buses to transport the people to the meeting at The Hill where the momentous decision on whether or not to fight was to be taken. Columbus, mindful of his position in the Education Department which forbade involvement in such activities, refused. The rebels believed this could only mean he was a collaborator, though Winnie was sure he must sympathize with the cause even though he felt he could not be a part of it. His family feared his refusal to co-operate with Intaba would result in his suffering the same fate as the chiefs and headmen who had been killed. Many of the rebels who had escaped the police were in hiding in a nearby forest. Calling themselves the Horsemen, they would creep out at night to exact retribution from collaborators.

Aware that he was a target for punishment, Columbus made preparations to be given warning of an attack and he remained alert at night. When the Horsemen did come he heard them approaching and made good his escape through a back window of his house. That escape remains something of a miracle to Winnie as her father was a big man and the window seemed impossibly small for him to have squeezed through. But escape he did and the attackers, finding their quarry had fled, went to a nearby hut where Winnie's grandmother was sleeping. The old woman was beaten up and left for dead. She survived but was paralysed for the rest of her life.

Jeremiah told Winnie that the trouble was continuing. Now the tribesmen had devised a scheme to boycott the stores of white shopkeepers who were unsympathetic towards them. For more than a year, says Winnie, the government proved implacable over its plans in the face of widespread Pondo opposition. Nearly 5,000 people were arrested. Yet, when a handful of white traders, dependent on the Pondos for their livelihood, complained of the effect the black boycott was having on them, the government agreed to make concessions to the Pondos in return for a lifting of the boycott on the trading stores. One of these concessions was that the Land Trust scheme was never enforced in Pondoland though the state of emergency continued.

As a direct result of the attack on him Columbus made a momentous decision that Winnie heard about only later—at first with disbelief and later with rage. He joined Kaiser Matanzima in putting into effect the South African government's scheme of fragmenting the country into ethnic areas to be known as homelands, with the Transkei being singled out as the first for "independence".

Matanzima had pointed out to Columbus that it was a natural progression for a Bunga councillor to join the Transkei government-to-be. Columbus resigned his teaching post and joined Matanzima's "cabinet" in what was to be a limited form of self-government under strict white supervision. (So-called independence was only declared many years later, in 1976, but has never been recognized outside South Africa.) Columbus assisted in drawing up all the clauses for the new constitution and was given the title of Minister of Agriculture and Forestry, an important portfolio in a part of the country almost entirely dependent on the land. The major part of the income needed to run the puppet state was to come from the South African government as an inducement to comply with the dumping of thousands of blacks from the cities in the already poverty-stricken Transkei.

Winnie had had no inkling of the direction in which her father's thoughts had been turning. Although his decision was a terrible shock to her and was to cause a rift in their close relationship, she always defends him, maintaining that Columbus was genuinely misled into thinking that by joining Matanzima he was going to liberate the people. Her loyalty to her father was vindicated years later when he changed his opinion and admitted, before he died, that he had been mistaken in believing the plan to move towards independence would be best for the Transkei. By then he had seen the consequences in the run-up to coming independence— thousands of blacks uprooted from their homes in urban areas and dumped in the Transkei without money or jobs, some of them never having seen the area before, and all Transkeians to be deprived of their South African citizenship. The continuing poverty in the Transkei and condemnation by the outside world were other factors that caused him to change his mind.

While worrying about the Pondo revolt and about Nelson's detention after Sharpeville, Winnie discovered she was pregnant again. Though Zeni was still a baby, Winnie was pleased to be having another child so soon, as she sensed there might be no opportunity to have more children in the future. This premonition proved to be true. One of her big regrets today is that she did not have the chance to have more children. She sent word to Nelson, detained in the Johannesburg Fort, that he was to become a father again towards the end of the year.

No doubt because of all her worries, this second pregnancy did not go as smoothly as the first. Winnie suffered particularly from nausea which became so distressing that she sought the help of Dr Motlana. He decided to give her an injection of sparene which he believed to be an innocently humble drug.

"That action proved to be one of the most frightening experiences I have ever encountered in my practice," recalls Dr Motlana. "I thought I was simply giving her an anti-hermetic drug, but she collapsed on the spot—no discernible pulse, nothing! My first reaction was to carry her to my car and get her to hospital but I needed help so I called in two of my colleagues. One of them said: 'What have you done? You have killed Mrs Mandela,' but fortunately the other one had had experience of the drug I had used. He knew that a few people were allergic to sparene and obviously Winnie was one of them. She recovered completely but that is an experience I can never forget."

Throughout this time Winnie was continuing her work for the Child Welfare Society, putting aside her own nagging worries under a cheerful exterior while she absorbed herself in the troubles of others. One of her sisters was staying at the house at Orlando West and she was able to leave little Zeni with her during office hours. Her real harassment had not yet begun, for the authorities probably believed her enforced dismissal from Baragwaneth Hospital would prove a salutary enough lesson to deter her from other political activities. Now that Nelson was out of the way in detention they no doubt thought that Winnie, deprived of his influence, could be manipulated to toe the line. They vastly underestimated her, as they were to realize in the years ahead.

Nelson was still in detention when the time came for him to give evidence at the Treason Trial in August 1960. The defence legal team had withdrawn temporarily from the case (they returned later) maintaining that they could not conduct a defence in a political trial under a state of emergency. So Nelson and his advocate friend and co-accused,

Duma Nokwe, took over the defence until the original team felt able to return.

Winnie was in court when Nelson gave evidence, and though she knew him so well and knew what he intended to say she was as spellbound as any who heard him. His evidence-in-chief and cross examination filled 441 pages of the court record. Many believe it was his sound reasoning and outstanding exposition of the ANC's views and actions that brought the calibre of his leadership to widespread notice in the world outside.

The trial continued and at the end of August, when the state of emergency was lifted, Nelson was released from detention. Over the months those detained had been let out in batches, a few at a time, while the authorities tested popular reaction. Nelson was among the last to be freed, five months after he had been detained. Winnie subdued her fears for the future in the joy of having Nelson home again for even a brief period. He had to make the 40-mile journey to court in Pretoria each day, but Winnie could drive off to work happy in the knowledge that he would be back home for dinner that night—a simple pleasure that she knew might soon be denied her for ever.

In December a phone call came through from the Transkei, where one of Nelson's sons by his first marriage was staying with the Matanzimas, to say the boy was ill. Nelson was distracted. He told Winnie he would just have to fetch the child for proper medical attention in Johannesburg. "But will they release you from your banning order to go?" queried Winnie. "I won't ask them," he replied.

Nelson drove through the night, picked up his son and travelled back to Johannesburg with no one in authority even knowing he had been gone. But in his absence Winnie went into labour. This time her confinement was to be in the Bridgeman Memorial Hospital where her sister Nancy had trained. Winnie's labour was a long and agonizing one, so different from Zeni's birth. The baby, another girl, born by forceps delivery on 23 December, was fine, but Winnie was very ill. She developed complications: puerperal fever set in and by the time Nelson arrived back in Johannesburg with his son she was running a high temperature and tossing and turning in distress.

Nelson dashed round to the hospital, upset at having missed this second birth, too. When he saw Winnie's condition he was incensed at what he believed was caused by neglectful treatment of his wife. He gathered up Winnie and the new-born baby in his arms—disregarding the warnings that she was too sick to be moved—and carried them out to his car. Back home he called in Dr Motlana to attend them and Winnie made a rapid recovery. The new baby was called Zindziswa, meaning "settled", but once again Winnie had no part in the choosing of the name, which was the prerogative of a chief of the Thembu royal house.

Before long Winnie was able to return to her work at the Child Welfare Society but she now had two babies to care for as well as Nelson to cosset before and after his hours at court. Another task she undertook was to find suitable schools for her two stepsons. Nelson was anxious that they should be out of harm's way if he were to be imprisoned for a long period so it was decided to put them as boarders to Anglican schools in Swaziland—the elder to St Michael's and the younger to St Christopher's.

All those who knew Winnie at that time marvelled that she managed to cope so well without breaking under the strain. She would rise early, pack the children into the back of the car and drive to Kliptown, not far from Orlando West, to drop Zeni with friends there. Then it was on to Fordsburg to the home of Paul and Adelaide Joseph, two Indian friends who lived within easy reach of Winnie's office at Child Welfare. Adelaide Joseph had small children too, and she had offered to care for Zinzi in the day while Winnie was working. This help was not one-sided, for Adelaide had a handicapped son and Winnie, who specialized in paediatric social work, was able to give a great deal of help in the care of the boy. Both Winnie and Adelaide speak glowingly of the help each received from the other. The women had much in common. They had been married within a month of each other and Paul Joseph had been one of the original Treason Trialists with Nelson, though he was among one of the early batches of accused to be discharged from the case.

Each day after settling her daughters Winnie would go about her case-work in the Soweto townships and whenever she could she would drive to Pretoria to see how the Treason Trial was progressing. Eventually came the day, in March 1961, when judgement was due to be delivered on the 30 accused still facing charges.

Winnie was in court. Outwardly composed and unconcerned, she sat waiting to hear the verdict. No one seeing her sitting there, so erect, calm and confident, smiling encouragement to Nelson and his colleagues, could have guessed the turmoil she was experiencing. What if it were to be the death penalty? Winnie shied away from the thought, as she had done a thousand times in the past few years since her marriage. She had steeled herself to hear the worst unflinchingly, so she could hardly believe her ears when Mr Justice Rumpff, telling the men in the dock to stand, said to them: "You are found not guilty and discharged."

The crowd went wild, cheering, dancing, weeping and singing the African national anthem—"Nkosi Sikelel' iAfrika"—which means "God Bless Africa". When Nelson and Winnie embraced in an ecstasy of joy and relief it was in the knowledge that things were just beginning, not ending. Now they would be able to continue the struggle within the country. While he received congratulations all round Nelson urged Winnie to go on home without him as he had to hold a meeting with his advisers. Winnie drove back to their home in Orlando West where a jubilant crowd thronged the house to celebrate the acquittal.

Walter Sisulu, Nelson's mentor, friend and fellow Treason Trialist, arrived and sought out Winnie, telling her to pack a suitcase with some clothing and essentials for her husband for a long absence. "I did not even ask why," says Winnie with engaging naïvety. But she did know that the ten years of bans on Nelson's movements and attendance at meetings had expired and that he wanted to make use of his "freedom" from restrictions before the authorities woke up to the fact that the bans had expired. While feigning ignorance of her husband's plans, Winnie left her guests to pack for Nelson. She handed over the luggage to Sisulu whom she calls "Uncle Walter" without, she avers, voicing any curiosity. Afterwards she returned to her friends to continue the celebrations without revealing that Nelson would not be coming home.

The next news of Nelson was that he had surfaced in Pietermaritzburg, the historic capital of Natal, close to Durban, where he was produced as the surprise speaker at a conference attended by 1,400 delegates from all over the country. At this time the government was preparing for the establishment of a republic after a referendum among whites only had approved such a move. Delegates at the conference demanded the holding of a national convention to draft a new constitution without a colour bar but, knowing this had no possibility of being granted, they called for country-wide demonstrations and a three-day stay-at-home to coincide with the establishment of a republic on 31 May, till then known as Union Day.

Nelson electrified the conference. Obviously he has a great sense of the theatrical because he appeared on the platform barefoot—a man of the people. And the people loved it. It became obvious that he was the leader of the ANC and he was unanimously elected to head the National Action Council charged with organizing a strike when efforts to force a convention failed. For Nelson this meant operating in secret, abandoning his legal practice and sacrificing his home life. He knew it was inconceivable that the authorities would allow him to operate freely without imposing a stringent banning order. Afterwards he said he could not have gone underground without the inspiration, courage and support of his wife.

At home in Soweto, where she waited with her two daughters, Winnie was told that after the meeting Nelson had disappeared and in future he would be working in secret, keeping in touch whenever he could. Though she expressed surprise at this news, she and Nelson had discussed just such a possibility and worked out many of the arrangements that followed. Nevertheless, it was frightening to know that it would be impossible now for Nelson to return without being arrested. Winnie tried hard not to give way to depression, which threatened to sap her vitality now that Nelson was not there to sustain her. Then, just when she was at her loneliest and most despondent, one visitor among the streams who called to sympathize and console her struck a chord. He was an Anglican priest, the Revd Leo Rakale. His ministrations proved such a consolation to Winnie that she joined the Anglican Church, and her faith has sustained her to this day. Religion had been a strong influence in her childhood and Mr Rakale, she says, brought her back to the fold. Her friend Helen Joseph was a staunch Anglican and this may well have influenced Winnie's decision, for by now she and Helen were close friends.

Mrs Joseph, like Winnie, had led a life of harassment during sixteen years of banning. She too suffered many personal attacks. Her gate was booby-trapped with explosives, she received death threats and was the butt of many cruel jokes. She is still a listed person, which means, in South Africa, someone who is deemed by the Minister of Justice to be a communist, but her banning order was lifted in 1973 after she had had an operation for cancer and her plight had evoked worldwide protests about her treatment.

Winnie, as well as being a devout Anglican, is a great believer in the ecumenical movement. She is glad to accept counsel, she says, from people of any religion—Protestant, Roman Catholic, Jewish, Muslim or Hindu. It is one of the most striking things about her that she inspires loyalty from so many people of such diverse origins, all implacably opposed to the system in South Africa.

The year and a half that followed Nelson's "disappearance" underground was fraught with anxiety for Winnie. She anticipated each secret meeting with him with fearful longing, desperate to see him but equally desperate that by meeting him she should not give him away. In spite of being in hiding Nelson made his presence felt throughout the country, travelling widely to explain the situation to the people and conducting his own propaganda campaign since the only way of keeping the masses informed of ANC activities was by word of mouth. He kept popping up where least expected in far-flung parts of the country, much to the chagrin of the security police who had a huge drag-net out for his capture.

Winnie had only to open her *Rand Daily Mail* each morning to find out where Nelson had surfaced and how he had eluded the police once again. The reports began to read like an exciting serial. He managed to travel the length and breadth of the country in secret, telling people in the cities and the remote rural areas of developments in the banned ANC. Thanks to the clothing his wife had packed for him and to his tailor, a Mr Khan, he became known as the best-dressed revolutionary. Because of his height and extremely long legs Nelson could not buy his clothes off the peg, so his suits were of necessity tailor-made, and extremely smart. His elusiveness in the face of countless traps set for him by the police added to his picture as a legendary figure. Inevitably the press came to refer to him as the Black Pimpernel. The security police watched Winnie like a hawk. They were convinced that Nelson, who was so attached to his family, would attempt to see his wife and children. But both Nelson and Winnie were aware of the dangers and they took all the precautions necessary to elude the watchers. They were a formidable team, even against the extremely efficient South African Police.

With the help of good friends, the use of stand-ins and careful planning by the ANC, the couple were able to meet many times. The fact that so many secret trysts were arranged successfully in the face of such constant surveillance remains quite one of the most remarkable aspects of the situation.

Because those meetings involved so many others who might still suffer if their actions became known, Winnie will not disclose details of the sometimes hair-raising schemes they devised. But one of the channels used by the ANC was made possible through the help of two friends, Harold and Ann-Marie Wolpe, who later settled in England. Harold, an attorney now turned academic, at present heads the Sociology Department of the University of Essex.

The Wolpes first met Winnie when Nelson started dating her. She seemed to them then to be very shy and it is easy to see why, for her natural exuberance is often disguised until she has summed up a new acquaintance. Later they came to appreciate her warm, outgoing personality.

"Nelson had a powerful effect on everyone who came in contact with him," says Harold. "I found it fascinating to watch him develop from a little-known lawyer into a political leader of great stature. Even as an awaiting-trial prisoner he made his personality felt. When I took him books he needed for the preparation of his defence he swept majestically into the interview room at the prison, apologizing for not being able to offer me drinks or tea and behaving for all the world as though he were receiving guests. Taking the law books from me he would pass them nonchalantly, with an offhand 'Do carry these for me will you?' to the white warders waiting like lackeys behind him. I was astonished to see the warders react with alacrity to do his bidding."

Many of the clandestine meetings between Winnie and Nelson took place at Lilliesleaf Farm in a Johannesburg suburb. This had been rented by a friend, Arthur Goldreich, as the headquarters of Umkhonto we Sizwe (Spear of the Nation). Umkhonto had been formed by Nelson and others because, they said, the ANC's peaceful protests over the past 50 years had always been met with violence by the government. Now Umkhonto would conduct a carefully controlled campaign of sabotage against installations, avoiding bloodshed. It was launched on 16 December 1961, with 23 acts of sabotage against economic targets.

The quiet suburb of Rivonia in which Lilliesleaf Farm is situated, was also an ideal meeting place for Winnie and Nelson. Their elder daughter, Zeni, though she was only a toddler at the time, retains an indelible impression of those hours spent with her father, being carried through the orchard in his arms, taken for a ride in a boat on the stream that ran through the farm, or just playing in the big, rambling house on the property. For years she refused to believe her father was in prison—insisting that he was living in the big house and would soon send for her to join him there.

One day Winnie was driving her car in the centre of Johannesburg when she pulled up at a red traffic light alongside a chauffeur-driven car. Glancing casually sideways as she waited, she was staggered to see that the chauffeur, uniform cap pulled well down over his eyes, was none other than Nelson. He was in one of his disguises designed to facilitate his movements as it enabled him to travel around by car to carry out his underground activities. In spite of her shock Winnie simply averted her eyes and gazed straight ahead, moving off quickly when the lights changed, as she was well aware that the slightest sign of recognition might well be picked up by the police who were never very far from her. Nelson, though he must have recognized his own car with his wife driving, remained impassive.

After ten months of moving around South Africa without being caught Nelson slipped away across the border to make a tour of African states. Every day now Winnie rushed to read the papers, all of which carried accounts from abroad of Nelson's movements and activities. He met a host of leaders including Julius Nyerere, Emperor Haile Selassie and the presidents of Sudan, Tunisia, Mali, Guinea, Liberia, Algeria and many others. Then he travelled to London to meet other influential people and finally to East Africa for talks with more leaders.

When he returned he told Winnie and his friends that what had struck him most forcibly on his travels (his first outside the land of his birth) was the sight of blacks and whites mixing freely and amicably, something that brought home to him more than anything else the intolerable situation in his own country, where blacks were simply a workforce, regimented and controlled in every aspect of their lives.

Once the police learnt that Nelson was so close, in East Africa, they had all the border posts fully manned and alerted for his possible return so they could grab him if he tried to re-enter the country. But again Nelson managed to elude them all and to slip quietly back into South Africa. In each place he visited he had obtained the national dress of that country to take back as a gift for his wife, so on his return she found herself with a host of exotic costumes to wear.

Back in Johannesburg Nelson stayed in a house right opposite the police station as he always held the view, rightly as it proved, that the police were least likely to look for him right under their own noses. But the net was closing, and both Winnie and Nelson knew it. Meetings became perilous, for now that the police knew Nelson was in Johannesburg they smartened up their efforts to find him. Following the frequent failures to trap Nelson, the South African government had called in the head of Britain's security services, Sir Percy Sillitoe, to help increase police efficiency, and he had advised them on methods of capture.

Seventeen months after he had gone underground Nelson had his final meeting with Winnie. It was the last time she was to have any physical contact with him for 22 years.

The journey for that final meeting is one she will always remember. Road blocks had been set up all around Johannesburg—a seemingly impenetrable net to trap Nelson—but Winnie managed to breach them. The plan was that she would pretend to be a woman far advanced in labour. She lay in an ambulance with her two little children beside her and a white-coated doctor, complete with stethoscope, in attendance (not, she emphasizes, one of her well-known medical friends). Groaning, writhing and even shrieking realistically, she was driven through the road blocks. The policemen who inspected the interior of the ambulance at each road block were completely taken in by Winnie's performance of a woman in pre-natal agony. How she and the children managed to get into the ambulance without being seen by the vigilant police watchers cannot be disclosed, though it is known that realistic stand-ins were used to put the authorities off the scent.

Soon after that family reunion at Lilliesleaf Farm an informer gave Nelson away. He was captured, on 5 August 1962, by three car-loads of armed police using methods advised by Sir Percy Sillitoe.

Chapter Eight

Now Dr Verwoerd's most wanted man—as Nelson had been dubbed during his seventeen months underground—was to face another trial, this time with scant hope of acquittal.

When word reached his home in the Transkei that he was to be charged with inciting African workers to strike (this referred to the March 1961 stay-at-home) and leaving South Africa without a valid travel document, a message was sent to Winnie that the tribal elders at Nelson's home wished to see her. She went at once, believing it was for a discussion of Nelson's predicament. To her dismay she was told that sessions had been arranged for her with a witch-doctor and she must undergo certain rituals to save her husband from conviction. Tribal superstitions of that kind were anathema to Winnie, whose strict religious upbringing in childhood had developed into firm Christian convictions in adulthood. She refused.

In retrospect she says it is one of the few decisions she regrets. Today she realizes that had she been more mature and had the sense that comes with experience, she would have thrown the bones to placate those relatives to whom such ritual meant so much. It would have done no harm and would have satisfied convention. As a result, she was blamed by some of Nelson's relatives for his imprisonment. It caused a great deal of ill-feeling which, fortunately, time and Winnie's future behaviour dissipated. It is an incident she finds hard to discuss. "I do not want to give the impression of a people still believing in that sort of rubbish," she says. "It might make people ask how we can hope to lead the country when that is the type of thing we believe. But superstition exists in every society and it was only afterwards, when I was older and wiser, that I realized how offensive it was to those in the tribe with age-old superstitions when I refused to throw the bones for the witch-doctor."

Nelson's trial was held in South Africa's administrative capital of Pretoria. In vain were objections made to the choice of a venue away from Nelson's home in Johannesburg. It was believed by his supporters

87

that Pretoria was chosen so as to limit the number of sympathetic spectators, who would find it difficult to travel all the way from Johannes-burg to lend their support at the trial. But in the event large numbers still attended.

Winnie herself made an unforgettable entrance to the courtroom, clad from head to foot in the striking beaded national dress of the Royal Thembu line. This so infuriated the authorities that the Minister of Justice served her with a notice banning her from the courtroom if she appeared again in tribal attire. That order backfired against the govern-ment, for when word of it spread among the people hundreds of black women turned up at the court on subsequent days wearing tribal apparel.

Winnie complied with the order, as she had no intention of being kept from the courtroom, but she wore instead clothing of black, green or yellow—the colours of the banned African National Congress: black for the people, green for the land and yellow for the gold beneath the ground. And on subsequent days she sported the outfits that Nelson had brought back to her typical of the countries he had visited. Nelson, too, caused a sensation. He strode into the dock, says Winnie, like an avenging giant, clad in a lionskin, symbol of a chief, given to him by his own paramount chief. His appearance was so striking that the entire courtroom, including the press, rose to their feet as he raised his fist and cried "Amandla" (meaning "power"). Throughout the days that fol-lowed he was heard with rapt attention, the complete silence around him testimony to the effect of his words.

Towards the end of his trial Winnie heard him say: "It has not been easy for me during the past period to separate myself from my wife and children, to say goodbye to the good old days when, at the end of a strenuous day at the office, I could look forward to joining my family at the dinner table, and instead to take up the life of a man hunted continually by the police, living separated from those who are closest to me, in my own country facing continually the hazards of detection and arrest . . . but there comes a time, as it came in my life, when a man is denied the right to live a normal life, when he can only live the life of an outlaw because the government has so decreed to use the law to impose a state of outlawry upon him. I was driven to this situation and I do not regret having taken the decisions I did take. . . ."

With sinking heart Winnie heard Nelson sentenced to five years' imprisonment with hard labour, three years for incitement to strike and two years for leaving the country without travel documents. But nothing would have induced her to give the police the satisfaction of seeing her upset at the sentence. Head held high, she joined other spectators in singing the moving anthem "Nkosi Sikelel' iAfrika". Afterwards she made a statement to *New Age*, a paper later banned by the Nationalist government.

"What has happened should take none of us by surprise, for we are faced with a vicious oppressor," she said. "I will continue the fight as I have in all ways done in the past." She added that her two daughters were too young to understand. "All the elder one knows is that her daddy was taken by the police. I shall cerrtainly live under great strain in the coming years, but this type of living has become part and parcel of my life. The greatest honour a people can pay to a man behind bars is to keep the freedom flame burning, to continue the fight."

Before Nelson began his sentence he was able to get to Winnie a letter he had written her in the awareness that they were to be parted for a long time. To Winnie it was the most wonderful letter any wife could receive, full of consolation, encouragement, inspiration and love. In it Nelson reminded his wife that this was what they had both expected to happen in their lives and he knew she would take it in her stride. He urged her to be strong and courageous and to remember what her position in the community must be in his absence. And, prophetically, he prepared her for difficult times ahead. She would have to bear the future without his protection and there would be many temptations deliberately put in her way. There would be traps, difficult to detect, and wolves in sheep's clothing of whom she should beware. There was bound to be slander, too, but she would have to face up to it all with courage. They had taken up a commitment to their people and this was the way of life they would have to endure.

There was much more wise and loving counsel. Winnie would dearly like to have that letter to re-read sometimes when she feels her spirits flagging, but that and every subsequent communication she received from Nelson in the early days was confiscated by the security police in raids on her home. In spite of frequent requests for its return it remains in police hands. "I suppose they have it in the police archives with other important papers," says Winnie with a laugh.

Many times in the months and years ahead she had cause to remember Nelson's prophetic warnings.

Soon after his arrest in August she was told that the police had started a rumour that Nelson was too old for her. The story was that as an attractive and glamorous young woman she could not face the prospect of spending her life tied to an imprisoned man nearly twice her age, so she had entered into a pact with the communists to hand him over to the police. Township talk, fostered by police informers, was that she had just married Nelson for his name and was looking around for another husband already.

Winnie was shocked by those stories. She could not understand how anyone could spread such vicious lies, but she was comforted by the thought that no one in the ANC who knew her would give credence to such a monstrous suggestion as the one that she had shopped Nelson herself. Those who knew Winnie realized the absurdity of such stories but rumours of just who had betrayed Nelson caused rifts between different groups.

Soon after Nelson's sentence came Winnie's first experience of the intrigue she was to encounter so frequently in the years ahead. He was still at the Johannesburg Fort, before his move to Pretoria and then to Robben Island, when Winnie was given a message that Moosa Dinath wanted to see her urgently at the Fort where he was serving a prison sentence. Dinath had been introduced to Winnie some time previously by Nelson who had known him for years, so when the message came she had no hesitation in going to the Fort to see what he wanted.

Dinath was an Indian who had married in Lourenço Marques (now Maputo) to circumvent the law which forbade intermarriage in South Africa. For the same reason his white wife went by her previous name of Maude Katzellenbogen. Maude seemed a good friend, always offering Winnie help in various ways. At the Fort, instead of being shown into the visitors' room, Winnie was taken to the administrative offices where Dinath was sitting with a senior prison officer. Winnie's first thought was that something had happened to Nelson and they had called her in to tell her about it. Seeing how shaken she looked Dinath assured her that Nelson was all right. Indicating the prison officer Dinath said: "He is here to prove to you that the plan I am about to unfold has his approval." The officer then left the room.

"Dinath proceeded to tell me an extraordinary story," recalls Winnie. "He said that his friend in the prison was prepared to let Nelson escape on condition he was paid £600 for doing so. He asked if I could raise the money. Obviously I could not raise even a quarter of that but I said nothing, realizing that he meant me to go to the ANC for the money. He said I should hurry because the escape had to be carried out before

Winnie arriving at court in the early sixties

Wedding day smiles

Winnie and Nelson after his release from detention following
the Sharpeville massacre

Winnie at home in Soweto with her two children

The Mandela family home in Soweto showing the protective wall

Winnie in the Transkei with Paramount Chief Sabata Dalindyebo

The Brandfort dwelling before Winnie transformed it

A grandmother at home—in her Brandfort garden with four of her five
grandchildren: Zaziwe, Zamaswazi; Zinhle and Zoleke

Unable to travel herself others collect honours on Winnie's behalf. Adelaide Tambo, left, accompanied Winnie's elder daughter, Zeni, to Haverford Quaker College in the USA for a ceremony at which Winnie was made an honorary doctor of laws.

Nelson was transferred to Pretoria from Johannesburg. Once the officer had received the £600 from me he would provide Nelson with a saw to cut through the bars of his cell. Nelson would be given a revolver, the prison doors would be opened for him and he would be allowed out safely. But, he added, the £600 must be paid first.

"My blood ran cold. That was one of the few occasions I was really worried about Nelson's safety. It was the first time it struck me that his life was at the mercy of the government.

"I was not yet accustomed to the dirty tricks of the security police but I recognized the absurdity of the scheme. Think of the noise of sawing through those iron bars. And how would it be possible for a man as well-known as Nelson, and of such huge stature, just to walk out of the Fort carrying a revolver? Obviously the plan was to allow him to saw through the bars of his cell and then to shoot him, justifying this by saying he was armed and killed while trying to escape. Although Nelson had told me Dinath was a friend'I could not imagine that he could have believed the scheme a genuine one and could not see there was some plot behind it."

In spite of her apprehension Winnie kept an impassive face and pretended to go along with the plan which Dinath kept insisting was foolproof. She did not have £6, much less the £600 being demanded, but she said she would see about raising the money and rushed from the Fort.

"I didn't sleep a wink that night," recalls Winnie. She realized she must get advice on the matter. Walter Sisulu was one man she knew she could trust to give her wise counsel. To him she poured out the whole story. Walter was appalled. He pointed out all the flaws in the scheme and told Winnie he was convinced it was a trap. "Do nothing and do not go back to the Fort. Leave it to me," he told her.

Winnie took his advice and soon Nelson was whisked away, first to Pretoria and then to Robben Island to do gruelling manual work in a limestone quarry on that bleak outcrop of rock in Table Bay, six miles off Cape Town, which was used to house prisoners. It was a hideous situation for a man of Nelson's ability and education to spend his days hacking at limestone. But at least he was alive. Winnie sincerely believed that Dinath was a tool and not a participant in the plot against Nelson so, believing he had been manipulated, she saw no reason not to trust his wife, Maude, who was going out of her way to foster her friendship with Winnie.

One of the many people associated with Winnie at this time was Mary

91

Benson, an English writer (later to become Nelson Mandela's biographer) who had been working as secretary to Chief Luthuli, President of the ANC and as secretary of the Treason Trial Defence Fund. She was soon to be deported, but in the meantime was doing what she could to help the liberation movement. One of her gestures was to provide the money for Winnie to buy a Gestetner machine on which to run off pamphlets and newsletters. Maude, hearing of this, offered to house the machine in a room at her own home.

"If you keep it the police will confiscate it next time they raid your house," said Maude. This seemed good sense to Winnie, so she installed the machine in Maude's house and did much of her work on it there. Maude also suggested that her address should be used rather than Winnie's own to receive mail from Nelson's overseas contacts. As letters to Winnie seldom reached her, she had devised cover names for her mail from abroad. She now gave Maude's address for them. Later she was to discover that the police had detailed information about the pamphlets and the cover names.

The previous year she had been invited to a multi-racial party at the *Rand Daily Mail*. There she had met Gordon Winter, a journalist who professed to be very sympathetic towards blacks and their struggle. As it happened Winter was one of the most successful spy recruits of the South African Bureau for State Security (BOSS). Part of his strategy was to help a few blacks to escape from South Africa and then to be deported to England himself, supposedly for his subversive activities, thus gaining a foothold among ANC activists abroad. He cultivated Winnie assiduously and she came to regard him as a friend. Certainly not all his friendliness was a charade, for much later he admitted liking Winnie enormously and admiring her spirit even while betraying her. But, as he described in his book, *Inside BOSS*, he winkled out of Winnie her cover addresses and the names of people working with her in the ANC which he passed on to the police.

In spite of having access to Winnie's mail and to the pamphlets she was producing, the security police were obviously worried by now that she was managing to conduct anti-apartheid activities of which they knew nothing. They decided she must be stopped. Not long after the start of Nelson's five-year sentence they arrived at 8115 Orlando West to serve her with a banning order. Two years earlier Helen Joseph had become the first woman in South Africa to have a banning order imposed on her. Nelson had been banned for years so Winnie knew just what it meant.

Her ban restricted her to the magisterial area of Johannesburg which she could not leave without permission; it prohibited her from entering any educational premises (not even to take her children to school) and it forbade her to attend or address any meetings or gatherings of more than two people. It was a harsh ban, but she was still able to go to work to earn the money so desperately needed to keep her family now that Nelson was behind bars.

Beset with her own troubles, Winnie still found time to help others in need. Nelson's close associates were either in exile or in hiding, so it was often Winnie who was approached for assistance by those in trouble. One of those the police were seeking was Nelson's secretary at his legal practice, Ruth Mompati. Acting on instructions Ruth had gathered up all Nelson's files and vacated his offices before the police pounced. She and Winnie were still very close and it was to Winnie that Ruth turned for help in escaping the police net.

Remembering her husband's dictum that the closer the danger the safer the hiding place, Winnie took Ruth into hiding in her own home in Orlando West even though it was under constant surveillance by the police. Each day when she left for work with her two daughters in the car she would lock up the house as though it were empty while inside Ruth would be working on Nelson's legal files: winding up those she could and handing the unfinished cases on to other solicitors.

While Ruth was alone in the house one day several men arrived in a furniture van demanding admission. They said they were from Levine's Furnishers and had come to repossess the furniture as the due instalment had not been paid. As was customary in South Africa Nelson had furnished his house on the hire-purchase system, but Winnie did not know this. His payments had lapsed when he was kept incommunicado in prison. Winnie says she received no warning notice that the goods were about to be repossessed and, though the bulk of the cost had been paid by then, every single item of furniture and furnishings was stripped from the house—even the lino on the kitchen floor was ripped up and carted away, leaving only clothing, bedding, books and utensils behind. Repossession was not an unusual occurrence in South Africa and particularly in Johannesburg, where hire-purchase sharks persuaded blacks to buy expensive furniture beyond their means, without making sure they understood the prohibitive interest charges. When they defaulted on payment, believing the total to have been paid, the goods would be repossessed. So many iniquitous cases have been publicized in the

English language press that recently the government introduced legislation to tighten up the hire-purchase laws.

Winnie had a telephone in her house so Ruth, agitated at this unexpected intrusion, phoned her at the Child Welfare Society offices to warn her of what had happened so she had all day to absorb the shock. Facing up to a crisis alone was something the ever-resourceful Winnie was learning to do. There was no way she could contact Nelson, so she knew she would have to accept that the furniture had gone for good. Life had seldom looked more daunting than when she returned to the empty house that evening with her two babies, knowing that the children and Ruth looked to her for support and that she must be strong, though all she really wanted to do was to weep for Nelson's comforting presence. Forcing back her tears, she borrowed a brazier from a neighbour because even her stove had been removed. She lighted a fire in the brazier and warmed some food for her children—persuading Ruth to join her in eating something. Afterwards she spread blankets on the floor, on which the two women and two children slept huddled together.

Overnight Winnie had worked out a solution. The next day she approached Godfrey Pitje, a lawyer who had been articled to Nelson and who owed Nelson several favours. She asked him to lend her the money to replace the repossessed furniture. He did so. Winnie bought enough furniture to carry on and she skimped from her salary for a long time to pay him back every penny.

Soon afterwards Ruth escaped across the border and after many vicissitudes ended up in London where she worked for the ANC for many years before her transfer to Lusaka. For Winnie it was yet another friend gone from her horizon, but she could not begrudge Ruth her chance to reach safety. Soon the security police began raiding Winnie's home almost daily and Ruth would certainly have been arrested if she had remained.

Winnie became inured to the loud bashing with truncheons on the door before dawn—the prelude to yet another raid. Rough hands would sling her possessions about, guttural Afrikaner voices sneering at her in resentment of her disdainful expression as she watched them pawing through her belongings.

In the years to come Winnie was to be the butt of prolonged vindictive treatment from the security police. She was spared physical violence because she was now so well known that any evidence of physical harm would, as the police realized, have aroused an outcry. But on one occasion her arm was broken by two young police reservists who did not know her identity.

At that time Paul Joseph, husband of Winnie's friend, Adelaide Joseph, was in detention in Mondeor Police Station. Winnie lived much closer to Mondeor than Adelaide, whose home was in the Indian area of Fordsburg, so she arranged to take food to Paul on Adelaide's behalf on alternate days. When she walked into the police station with a plate of food and stated who it was for, the two young Afrikaner reservists on duty decided to have some sport with her. Not knowing who she was they asked her why a kaffirmeid (African girl) was taking food to a koelie (Indian). Their taunting turned to scuffles and in the ensuing affray Winnie's arm was broken. She refused to leave until she had seen the station commander and eventually one of the reservists picked up the phone and told the officer there was a kaffirmeid insisting on seeing him. When the station commander walked in and saw that the kaffirmeid was actually Mrs Mandela he was aghast. He allowed her to lay a charge against the men for assault, but later she was notified that the Attorney General had declined to prosecute.

Now that Nelson was out of the way and unable to use his legal knowledge to protect his family and protest against injustices meted out to them, the security police campaign against Winnie increased. Little Zeni was now a toddler and her mother, determined that the child should not receive the inferior education that was provided for blacks in government schools, placed the little girl in a fee-paying Roman Catholic nursery school in Kliptown nearby. The child was delighted with her first school but when she had been there only four days a letter arrived for Winnie from the nuns saying they regretted that they could not keep Nelson Mandela's child at their school. The nuns had been aware of who Zeni was when they accepted her, so Winnie knew they must have been instructed by the security police to reject their new pupil.

Though far worse measures were to be taken against Winnie personally in the years to come, she still believes that that police action against her innocent little daughter was the most iniquitous of all. She came perilously near to showing her despair. Instead, she managed, with the help of her Indian friends, Paul and Adelaide Joseph, to place Zeni in an Indian kindergarten. It was a privately run school, which was how a black child was able to attend. In government schools strict segregation starts at a very early age in South Africa: white, Indian, black and coloured (mixed race) each being confined to their own schools. Recently some private schools have admitted a few non-white pupils but high fees prevent any but the very wealthy from attending. Thus the intake of blacks is pitifully small.

In all the years her children were of school age Winnie was unable to meet any of their teachers to have a discussion about their work, nor was she ever able to attend prize-givings, sports, parent-teacher meetings or other activities connected with her daughters' schooling—something, she says, that has left a big gap in her life.

In June 1963, Winnie was given permission to visit Nelson on Robben Island for 30 minutes. That half-hour visit entailed a journey of 900 miles from Johannesburg to Cape Town and then a ferry ride for the six-mile trip to Robben Island.

"It was horrible," Winnie recalls. "They had built a clumsy shelter right on the shore with double wire mesh separating prisoner and visitor on each side. They brought Nelson down to this enclosure and I had to stand opposite him for the entire half-hour. All I could see of him was his silhouette. There was nowhere to sit. We had to talk very loudly to be heard at all, and with the white warders standing alongside us listening to every word it was most embarrassing. They warned us that we had to speak either English or Afrikaans—Xhosa was forbidden in case we said something they did not understand. If we mentioned the names of anyone they interrupted and threatened to stop the visit. They were incredibly hostile. I was so depressed when I came away, but at least I had seen Nelson and he had appeared pleased and relieved to see me.

"At that time Nelson's jail conditions were appalling. The food was particularly bad and there were no privileges. We had to fight for every one of those over the years."

Back home Winnie found the police had ransacked her home again in her absence.

Throughout the sixties and seventies she was to be arrested frequently. She herself has lost count of the number of times this has happened but in one case alone she appeared in court nineteen times on the same charge before being acquitted. Often when she was found guilty in a lower court the conviction would be set aside when the case was taken on appeal, usually because of conflicting or flimsy evidence. All the efforts to find Winnie guilty of any criminal offence were in vain.

Chapter Nine

NELSON HAD BEEN on Robben Island for only a few months of his five-year sentence when the ANC received another crippling blow. An informer told the police about the existence of Lilliesleaf Farm in Rivonia which was being used as the underground headquarters of Umkhonto we Sizwe. In mid-1963 the police swooped on the farm, arresting Walter Sisulu and several other leading figures in the movement. Others were picked up later. Four of the men detained—Harold Wolpe, Arthur Goldreich, Mosie Moolla and Abdullah Jassat—succeeded in carrying out one of the most audacious jailbreaks of modern South African history.

Their arrest had been hailed by the government as a real coup and they were under close guard at Marshall Square Police Station in Johannesburg. But while the prosecution was preparing its case the four men were planning to escape. Arthur Goldreich noticed at exercise time that one of the young policemen acting as a warder, Johannes Greef, who was only eighteen, was looking particularly downcast. He drew the young man into conversation and elicited the reason for his misery—he had damaged a friend's car and had to find £50 for its repair. Goldreich sympathetically offered to get him the money but added that he would need to make a phone call to arrange it. That call alerted friends outside to the possibility of escape. By accepting the £50 Greef opened himself to bribery—something the prisoners were not slow to exploit. The two Indians, in particular, managed to establish a friendly relationship with Greef before offering him £2,000 if he would help them to escape. He agreed.

Now Harold's wife, Ann-Marie, brought into play the organizing ability that had aided Nelson and Winnie in planning many of their clandestine meetings when Nelson was in hiding. To her fell the task of working out the procedure once the men were outside Marshall Square. She arranged for a car to be waiting for them to take them into hiding in Johannesburg until it was safe for them to leave the country.

Others arranged where they should hide in the meantime so that Ann-Marie would know as little as possible if she were interrogated. To begin with the scheme succeeded without a hitch. The four men slipped out in the dead of night but it took them much longer to do so than they had anticipated, so the driver of the get-away car, thinking the plan had failed, gave up hope and drove off.

Dismayed that there was no transport waiting the fugitives nevertheless were determined not to give up. They decided to split into pairs, as two Indians walking with two whites in the street in the early hours would be a target of curiosity. Harold and Arthur set out on foot to reach one of the homes where they had been offered sanctuary. By a quite incredible coincidence that still amazes the men today a passing motorist who stopped to offer them a lift turned out to be a friend who readily agreed to drop them off at their destination and to say nothing of the matter to anyone. A similar stroke of luck aided the two Indians who met a waiter friend leaving his work and were taken to temporary safety. Then began the ordeal of waiting under cover till the hue and cry had died down. Harold and Arthur moved from house to house and finally holed up in a small empty cottage where they were afraid to strike a light for fear of attracting attention and scarcely dared move lest the noise caused someone to investigate who or what had got into the house. Ann-Marie was arrested the very next day and severely interrogated before being released 24 hours later. The wisdom of keeping her in ignorance of the get-away houses paid off.

The newspapers had a field day with reports of the escape and pictures of the wanted men. The police, furious at being outsmarted, were making extensive searches and keeping a vigilant watch on the border which they knew the men would have to cross to reach safety. Speculation and wild stories as to their whereabouts were rife. Eventually they were packed into the boot of a friend's car and driven to Swaziland. There, to avoid embarrassing the British authorities, they disguised themselves as priests and claimed they were visiting missions in Swaziland and Botswana for which they chartered a plane. Harold called himself the Revd Eric Shipton, a name he will never forget as it helped him to freedom. As bogus priests the men were eventually able to fly to England.

The unfortunate young warder was never able to collect his £2,000. He was arrested and sentenced to a jail term but before that he agreed, under interrogation, to trap the man bringing him the bribe money. Word of the treachery got out, however, and the rendezvous for the pay-off was never kept.

Winnie was relieved to hear that four of her friends had managed to escape but now, with shocked surprise, she heard that Nelson was being brought back from Robben Island to face trial with the others arrested at Rivonia. Among the literature confiscated at the farm by the police was sufficient evidence, it was said, of Nelson's implication to put him in the dock with the others. Winnie's mind was in turmoil. It would mean she would see Nelson again soon—if only in a courtroom—but it meant, too, the prospect of another sentence being added to the five years he was already serving.

In December, 1963, the trial of the men—which became known as the Rivonia trial—began in the Palace of Justice in Pretoria. At their first appearance some weeks previously their counsel, Bram Fischer, QC, later to become a political prisoner himself, had pointed out the vagueness and absurdity of the allegations, some of which accused Mandela of sabotage committed when he was on Robben Island and in which he could not possibly have taken part. The judge agreed and the men were acquitted, only to be immediately re-arrested. At their second trial they were accused of nearly 200 acts of sabotage and conspiracy to overthrow the government by revolution.

Now began a period of euphoria and despair for Winnie. She clubbed together with the relatives of the other accused to buy food to give to the prisoners each day. She felt revitalized every time Nelson smiled at her and spoke to her so encouragingly, if briefly, from the dock, and despair when she listened to the prosecutor, Percy Yutar, and realized that he was working up to demand the death sentence. But overseas, in the United Nations and elsewhere, sympathy for Nelson was widespread, and it was generally believed that the force of overseas opinion alone saved the men from the supreme penalty. Until the final judgement and sentence, though, Winnie was deeply apprehensive at the thought that Nelson might be hanged.

Her life at this time was under constant pressure. She would rise at dawn, dress and feed her children and drop them off on her way to her office. There she would begin her work before anyone else had arrived in order to be free to speed to Pretoria to listen to as much as she could of the case and exchange a few precious words with Nelson. Then it was the long rush back to Johannesburg to collect her children, who were being cared for by Adelaide Joseph, and be safely indoors by six o'clock to conform to her banning order.

For eleven months the trial, and Winnie's ordeal, continued. Nelson's conduct of the case and his reasoned arguments impressed a wide spectrum of people. Those who were in court to hear him were riveted by his articulate and forceful speeches, and the one memory of that time on which everyone there agrees is the utter silence in which Nelson was heard. There was no shuffling, no coughing, no whispering, no sound but Nelson's voice.

In his opening address he told the court that the suggestion by the state that the struggle in South Africa was under the influence of foreigners or communists was wholly incorrect. "I have done whatever I did, both as an individual and as a leader of my people, because of my own proudly felt African background and not because of what any outsider might have said," he added. He and others had formed the Spear of the Nation (Umkhonto we Sizwe), he said, because violence by the African people had become inevitable and unless responsible leadership was given to canalize and control their feelings there would be outbreaks of terrorism that would produce an intensity of bitterness and hostility between the races.

Because all the lawful modes of expressing opposition to white supremacy had been closed by legislation, blacks had chosen to defy the law without violence. Only when that method was legislated against and the government used force to crush any peaceful opposition to its policies did Umkhonto decide to answer violence with violence. But, said Nelson, this violence was not terrorism. Umkhonto's aim was to achieve liberation without bloodshed and civil clash. They had decided on sabotage because it did not involve loss of life and it offered the best hope for future relations as bitterness would be kept to a minimum. Winnie was in court with scores of supporters to hear his impressive statement which ended with the words:

"We want equal political rights because without them our disabilities will be permanent. I know this sounds revolutionary to whites in this country because the majority of voters will be Africans. This makes the white man fear democracy. But this fear cannot be allowed to stand in the way of the only solution which will guarantee racial harmony and freedom for all. It is not true that the enfranchisement of all will result in racial domination. Political division, based on colour, is entirely artificial

100

and when it disappears so will the domination of one colour group by another.

"The ANC has spent half a century fighting against racialism. When it triumphs it will not change that policy. Their struggle is truly a national one. It is a struggle of the African people, inspired by their own suffering and their own experience. It is a struggle for the right to live.

"During my lifetime I have dedicated myself to this struggle of the African people. I have fought against white domination and I have fought against black domination. I have cherished the ideal of a democratic and free society in which all persons live together in harmony with equal opportunities. It is an ideal which I hope to live for and achieve. But if needs be, it is an ideal for which I am prepared to die."

They were inspiring words and just what Winnie needed to hear to help her bear the increasing pressures she faced alone. As had been hoped, protests and pressure from overseas as the trial progressed saved the accused men from the death sentence. Instead they were given life imprisonment and life imprisonment in South Africa means just that, with no remission for political prisoners.

When sentence had been passed Nelson turned to wave to his wife and the crowd and that night was flown to Cape Town and taken by ferry to Robben Island, where he was to spend the next 20 years before being moved to a prison on the mainland in Cape Town, both places being almost as far away from Winnie as it was possible to keep him. Now she faced a long, bleak future alone. Her great consolation was her two little daughters. She was determined they should not suffer, becoming, if anything, over-protective towards them. This attitude was counterbalanced, however, by the number of times the two girls were to be parted from their mother in the years ahead.

After Zeni had spent a while at the Indian kindergarten both children were old enough to attend school so an arrangement was made for them to go to City and Suburban, a well-known school close to Winnie's place of work. This was a school for coloured (mixed race) children who were given a better education than black children. Winnie decided the risk of placing them there was justified on her offspring's behalf. A close relative of Nelson's, Judith Mtirara, who was lighter skinned than average, had put her own children to City and Suburban and she agreed to enrol Zeni and Zinzi with them under the surname of Mtirara. The Mandela girls were perfectly entitled to use that name as their father, through the extended family system of the Transkei, was entitled to take the names Matanzima, Dalindyebo and Mtirara as well as Mandela. During the period they were at the school an Indian friend of Winnie, Mrs "Amah" Naidoo, mother of detainees Indris and Shanti Naidoo, cared for the children after school hours without payment.

All went well for a while and the Mandela children settled happily to their lessons. However, from the way the security police watched Winnie it was inevitable they would soon realize her children were at a coloured school, something definitely prohibited to black children. One day after Judith had dropped them at school she was arrested by the security police who interrogated the terrified woman until she admitted having arranged the Mandela girls' entry. She was deeply distressed at having admitted this and confessed to Winnie. But Winnie understood. She knew how daunting police methods could be. Zeni and Zinzi had to leave the school. For Winnie the one redeeming aspect of that affair was that the school principal took the trouble to contact her to tell her he had had nothing to do with the expulsion and that he had been aware, all along, of the children's identity but had decided to turn a blind eye to such an innocent deception.

The problem of how to protect her children from further harassment was one that worried Winnie constantly in the weeks ahead. Though adversity had strengthened her and made her more self-reliant she often longed for someone close in whom she could confide. After the Rivonia trial the leadership of the ANC had been virtually eliminated, and those who were not in prison had fled the country—many of her close friends among them. Lonely and despondent, Winnie felt as though she were living in limbo, existing from day to day, almost without purpose and uncaring about anything except the fate of Nelson and her children. At night she would visualize Nelson labouring on that bleak outcrop of rock, lashed for most of the year by vicious winds.

It was her father who succeeded, unwittingly, in shaking her out of this unaccustomed, despairing lethargy. Her siblings at home in Pondoland had heard how she was feeling and one of her younger brothers, Msuthu, who had recently matriculated, went to Johannesburg to stay with Winnie. He took a job in the city in market research and was doing well at his work. The joy of Winnie's reunion with her brother, however, was to be short-lived. When the police raided her home they discovered the presence of Msuthu. Where, they wanted to know, was his permit to be in Johannesburg when he should be living in Pondoland? Msuthu, like millions of other blacks, was to become a victim of influx control—a law restricting the movement of blacks with the aim of keeping them out of "white" cities. He was arrested and charged with being in an urban area without valid documents. The newspapers, always on the lookout now for news about Winnie, seized on this new angle with glaring headlines reading: "Son of Transkei Minister of Agriculture Arrested."

Msuthu's arrest, conviction and fine and the publicity surrounding it led to the first and only violent row that Winnie and her father ever had. Columbus telephoned Winnie from his government offices in Umtata. Winnie knew the call was being monitored because an Afrikaner voice kept interjecting. Her father accused her of making political capital out of his son and subjecting him to unnecessary public glare. All Winnie's long-pent-up feelings erupted in fury at her father's attitude. For the first time in her life she cast aside her deference to Columbus. She told him that though he had chosen the narrow path of selling the birthright of his people in the Transkei none of his children had any obligation to toe the line of a puppet state. Columbus warned her that she would regret those words. Winnie retorted that, on the contrary, it was he who would rue his actions.

So incensed was she at her father's attitude that she followed up the telephone conversation by sending him a telegram confirming what she had said. Later her stepmother, Hilda, told her that Columbus had been so upset by this rift with his favourite daughter that he took to his bed for a whole week.

But in Winnie's case it had the effect of galvanizing her into action once again. Now she felt able to shake off her despair and act as Nelson would wish. She was still employed at the Child Welfare Society and this, with her political work, of which she was now picking up the threads, absorbed all her energies in the daylight hours. It was the nights that were the worst. Few blacks had telephones but several of Winnie's white friends, realizing the loneliness Winnie must be experiencing after dark, would ring for a chat to cheer her up. They knew her phone was tapped so conversations had to be kept to personal and trivial matters. A frequent phone caller was Helen Joseph, whose own banning order gave her a fellow-feeling with Winnie that was fast developing into an affectionate and lasting friendship. Helen often remarked in the years ahead that she had come to regard Winnie as the daughter she never had.

At this time Winnie knew she was a target for police harassment but she was not yet aware of the extraordinary lengths to which the authorities would go to undermine her. It came as a great shock to discover that the Child Welfare Society had, for the past four years, been under constant government pressure for employing her. All the society's social workers were subsidized by the South African government but when Winnie joined the staff the government refused to include her, thinking no doubt, that this would result in her dismissal. Instead her full salary was paid out of the society's own hard-pressed funds. It was a measure of the high regard they had for Winnie's work that they did not hesitate to take on this burden, nor did they let Winnie know about it. It was only later that she came to hear of it.

Nelson's warning to Winnie that people would betray her and set traps for her was about to be borne out once again.

One of the first of these deceptions involved a man called Brian Somana, a journalist who had written favourable reports about Winnie and Nelson and whom she regarded as a friend. He was, however, extremely bitter towards Walter Sisulu who, he claimed, had taken him out of a well-paid insurance job and persuaded him to join *New Age* (a paper soon to be banned) and he was unable to make a good living from this. His enmity towards Sisulu, however, did not appear to extend towards the Mandelas, and during the Rivonia trial, when Nelson commissioned Winnie to go to the Transkei to see the chief and senior members of his family, Somana offered to drive her and Nelson's sister there in his car.

In the Transkei Somana sat in on the family discussions which had also been attended by one of Nelson's uncles, Jackson Nkosiyane. Discussion was frank and uninhibited as was usual at family get-togethers.

No sooner had the visitors returned to Johannesburg than Jackson was arrested on what Winnie calls a trumped-up charge of plotting to murder Kaiser Matanzima, something for which he served six years in prison. Not for one moment did Winnie, at that stage, suspect Somana of informing on or distorting their family discussions, though with hindsight she cannot understand her naïvety, for Somana suddenly came into a lot of money. He bought himself a new car and set himself up in a sweet distributing business, acquiring an office in the same building in which Nelson had practised law. And he gave Winnie's sister a clerical job in his new office. Winnie believed his sudden wealth must be due to his doing better at his work.

She often called at his office to visit her sister, now employed there. One day, being temporarily without transport, she was complaining that she had about a hundred Child Welfare files in her office and needed a car to carry them. Somana, who was listening, offered to pick her up with the files. She arranged a time, telling him to make certain it was after a certain hour because she was expecting an ANC colleague to call for some political documents and she must be there to hand them over.

As fate would have it her ANC colleague arrived much earlier than expected, collected the prohibited documents and departed safely. Then, just at the later time when he had been due to arrive, the security police pounced. They rushed into Winnie's office and searched it thoroughly, going through every confidential file, mostly adoption papers, but discovering nothing incriminating. And Somana failed to pick up Winnie as arranged so she went round to his office to tell her sister of the raid and of her narrow escape. While they were talking a white man knocked at the door asking for Brian. Although he was in plain clothes Winnie knew at once that he was a security policeman—to her there was something unmistakable about the breed—and his manner was so suspicious that the truth dawned on Winnie: Brian was an informer. The visitor left an envelope for Somana. Without compunction Winnie opened it and read the typewritten words: "Meet me at the same time at the same place." This confirmed her suspicions, and now many past events that had puzzled her fell into place.

She and others had been lectured by their leaders on how to behave in a situation where an informer had been discovered. On no account were they to ostracize the person once his identity was known, as it was better to keep him ignorant of the fact that he had been unmasked. Winnie tried hard to adopt such an attitude, but Somana must have detected a change in her for he took to calling at her house frequently on the slightest pretext and probing to discover what she knew. His visits became so frequent and annoying that she asked Joel Joffe, who was then her attorney, for his assistance in shaking off this informer and preventing him from pestering her at home. Joffe wrote to Somana threatening to take him to court. The result of this came later when Somana's wife launched an action suing her husband for divorce and citing Winnie as co-respondent.

"I did not believe that even the scummiest of informers could stoop so low," she says. She realized that this must be part of the smear tactics instituted by the security police to humiliate her so she applied to the Supreme Court for permission to intercede in the action. Her application was granted and she explained to the judge that it had become known to her and others that Somana was an informer for the security police and that the divorce action was intended to harm Nelson and her reputation and had no basis of truth to it whatsoever. The result was that the Somana couple announced that they were withdrawing the divorce proceedings—a tacit admission that Winnie had not been involved.

Soon came another vicious blow. So far Winnie's banning order had not prevented her from travelling about in her daytime work and activities. Now the security police decided to stop her from visiting the various townships in Soweto as she was required to do in the course of her work. They withdrew her banning order and substituted a much more stringent one prohibiting her from entering any township other than Orlando West in which she lived. Winnie knew at once what it meant. She would no longer be able to practise as a social worker.

The Director of the Child Welfare Society, Mary Uys, was in tears when, a week later, she told Winnie she would have to leave. "But you are not being fired—if your banning order is relaxed we will take you back," she said. Winnie appreciated this attitude all the more for she now learnt about her unsubsidized salary and realized that in a way it must have been a relief to the society not to have to continue with the burden of paying her full salary themselves.

Winnie had been filling in her lonely evening hours by studying by correspondence for a degree in social science (for which a sympathizer had provided the fees) and was determined to continue with this even though she could no longer carry on with her social work. There was, however, the very real problem of earning enough money to live. She knew she would have to find a job quickly and now began what she terms an endless journey into the white commercial field to seek work.

She found it in a furniture shop, working for a pittance but at least it provided money for food. Just a couple of months later, in August 1965, she was sacked without reason. That became the pattern in any job she started and she soon realized that the security police, determined to prevent her from working at all, were engineering her dismissals.

That December she was taken on as a clerk in a correspondence college for black journalists. There had been no trouble at the interview when she was engaged but when she started work the Afrikaner receptionist told her the police had been and she would only be allowed to continue working there if she agreed to divorce Nelson. Winnie could scarcely credit this but her employer kept asking her when she was getting a divorce. Then she received notification from the chief magistrate of Johannesburg that she could not continue in her present post because it violated her banning order which prevented her from entering educational premises.

Interference continued. Next she was taken on by an Indian dry cleaner who paid her R20 a week, more than any of the other places. However, she had only been working there for three weeks when the police arrived and accused the Indian owner of contravening the Factories Act. "In a back room," says Winnie, "he had a number of broken-down machines for fixing shoes and some old typewriters. The police counted these and said there were nine whereas under the Factories Act he was only entitled to have eight. They threatened to charge him unless he dismissed me so I left."

For a while Winnie assisted her attorney, Joel Carlson, for R10 a week until he found this attracted unwelcome police attention. A lump sum had been sent to another attorney, James Kantor, for distribution to the dependants of the Rivonia trial leadership, and Winnie was called in to collect her share. "They had rounded up everyone but when I saw how destitute some of the others were my conscience would not let me take anything," says Winnie.

Those were hard times when she had to rely on the charity of friends just to pay the rent and eat. But she had her favourite sister, Nancy, to console her. Both were forcibly separated from their husbands and were trying to make ends meet with two children each to care for. Nancy had married Sefton Vuthela who had been working at the University of the Witwatersrand when he was arrested for his political activities and banned. When charged with violating his banning order he decided to flee to neighbouring Botswana rather than be sent to prison. There he ran the Botswana Book Centre, or BBC as some jokingly called it, for Sefton made a point of stocking many books, banned in South Africa, that went far beyond the august British institution's normal political parameters.

Once established in Botswana he sent for Nancy and their two children, both of whom are now studying in America. An old friend of Winnie, Elija Msibi, smuggled Nancy across the border to join her husband. Winnie was relieved to hear her sister had reached safety but she sorely missed the camaraderie her sister had provided. "There were many times when there was hardly a morsel of food in our homes but Nancy always found a way of providing a meal and she was such a cheerful, happy person." Now desperate for work, Winnie took a position in a shoe shop for only R4 a week.

Through these lean times necessity drove her to become an expert at baking. Because of its cost bakery bread was out of the question so Winnie made her own for her children. It was a skill she had picked up in childhood from her domestic science-trained mother but she relearnt by trial and error till she was able to produce a perfect loaf. And when there was money for the ingredients she made cakes too—soon becoming well-known for her light hand at baking.

Two months after Nelson had been sent to Robben Island to begin his life sentence Winnie was given permission to visit him. Now that the island was housing so many political prisoners a proper visitors' section had been erected. There was a glass partition between prisoner and visitor who had to speak to each other on two-way phones. Warders stood alongside listening to every word and a tape recording was made of the conversations. "Just in case the warders miss something," says Winnie wryly. When she returned home it was to find her house had again been ransacked by the police.

Disturbing as Winnie found the invasions of her working life, they were as nothing compared to the terror to which her personal life was being subjected. She was bathing her two children one evening after dark when the silhouette of a man wielding a revolver appeared at her bathroom window. Fortunately her neighbours had been alerted to keep a wary eye open for intruders after several minor incidents, and one of them spotted the man as he climbed on boxes to the bathroom window, scaring him off with his shouts. The police were called but, though there were plentiful fingerprints on the windowsill, no arrest was made.

Soon afterwards Winnie came to a decision that she had been balking at for some time but which she knew she could not put off any longer. She must protect her daughters from official vindictiveness. The only solution was to send them away to a school where they would be safe from harassment and free from the constant worry of seeing their mother raided and arrested. Finding a school for them when she was not allowed to leave Johannesburg was a problem. Because of the way the security police acted against people who helped her, many found it politic to stay out of her way now that Nelson and his close associates were all in jail or exile. But one old friend, Elija Msibi, who had engineered Nancy's escape, solved the problem for Winnie.

He was one of the few friends, she says, who at that parlous time was prepared to stick his neck out by offering to assist, even though he knew so many of Winnie's helpers had been detained. Elija was a wealthy man.

He had had no schooling and was quite illiterate but he had become a Soweto shebeen tycoon. For many years blacks were forbidden to buy—or drink—European liquor. All that was available to them was "kaffir beer" made from mealie meal. (It was ironic that while this prohibition existed the government condoned the custom on the Cape wine estates whereby coloured workers were often kept in a state of semi-drunkenness by the iniquitous system of paying part of their wages in tots of fortified wine.) The ban on blacks buying hard liquor had the inevitable result—illegal dens, known as shebeens, sprang up in all the townships. They sold not only the prohibited spirits but also shimiyane or skokiane, a ferociously strong illicit spirit often laced with such poisonous additives as car battery acid.

When prohibition ended the shebeens continued to flourish. They were the only venues where socially inclined blacks could drink, other than in their own homes or in the beerhalls which were restricted to the sale of traditional beer. The shebeens were allowed to operate since they provided plentiful pickings for the police informers who riddled black society. Blacks regarded the shebeens as a necessity and they became something of what the pubs are to the English working man. They thrived and so did the shebeen keepers and in particular Elija, who was one of the most successful of all the tycoons. But wealth did not turn him from his people and both then and in the future troubles he was to help Winnie and many others, using his illiteracy to disguise his covert activities and his wealth to help others in need.

It was he who solved the education problem for Winnie by travelling to Swaziland to find a school that would take the Mandela girls. Not only did he do this but he arranged to put his own daughters there so that Winnie's two could accompany his to and from Swaziland. To send her daughters away to a neighbouring country was a heartbreaking decision for Winnie to have to make. Though she always adopted a carefree, happy demeanour—a front lest the authorities should think they were succeeding in their attempts to intimidate her—she was desperately worried about the children. Apart from the vindictive way they had been hounded from two schools, Zeni and Zinzi had been torn from their mother on each occasion when she was arrested for allegedly breaking her banning order; there were constant raids on her home and although there were always willing relatives around to take care of them Winnie never knew from day to day when she would be taken away and have to leave them crying for their mother.

109

She steeled herself to send them away though Zinzi was only six years old. They wept bitterly at having to leave their mother and Winnie believes it was distress at the parting that caused her to develop the hyper-tension and heart condition that have plagued her ever since.

Unfortunately the Swaziland school chosen by Elija proved a bad choice. It was called the Convent of Our Lady of Sorrows. Winnie and her daughters all say it could not have been more appropriately named. Zeni and Zinzi remember it with horror. They found it a place of harsh, rigid discipline where they were bullied unmercifully and were miserably unhappy. No doubt being deprived of their mother's love served to make the place seem to them worse than it was. Winnie had agreed to a Roman Catholic institution, even though nuns had turned her little daughter away a few years before, as she was at her wits' end to find somewhere safe for them to be educated. Neither she nor Eljia could have known that the convent was to prove so unsatisfactory.

Alone now and determined not to give way to depression, Winnie joined a scheme to organize correspondence study courses for Nelson and other Robben Island prisoners. These had been started by students of the University of the Witwatersrand but they were ordered by the authorities to desist and another group took over. One of the prime movers was Sir Robert Birley, former headmaster of Eton College, who was a visiting professor at the University of the Witwatersrand. He and his wife, Elinor, met Winnie at the sessions to arrange the study courses. The two women became friends and have remained so. Since her husband's death Lady Birley has kept in touch from her retirement home in Somerset. It was to her that Winnie poured out her doubts about the Swaziland convent and later it was Lady Birley who suggested and arranged for the two girls to attend Waterford, an exclusive school in Swaziland. The fees were far beyond what Winnie could afford but Lady Birley and Helen Joseph provided the necessary money. Generous friends also paid the fees of Nelson's two sons, Father Hooper of St Michael's shouldering some of the burden himself.

At this time few people in South Africa knew of—or realized—Winnie's plight so it was left to a small circle of close friends to rally round. As long as Lady Birley remained in Johannesburg she did her best to cheer up Winnie (who, to outward appearances, needed no cheering) usually calling at the shop where she was working to take her out to lunch as she could not see her after hours.

Winnie has never been able to fathom why the police should waste so much time, effort and money on concocting trivial charges against her that invariably failed. There was the time she was woken at four in the morning to be arrested and, as she narrated in court, had closed her bedroom door to prevent the white detective sergeant watching her put on her underwear. He in turn told the court she pushed the bedroom door shut in his face and he thought she was going to lock it so he pushed it open and told her to follow him immediately. When she refused he said he would have to use force and grabbed her arm. She was charged with resisting arrest, but two months later was acquitted because of contradictory evidence.

Another charge followed an obvious misunderstanding on one of her rare visits to Cape Town to see her husband. When she alighted from the ferry someone called out asking her address.

"I thought he was a reporter," recalls Winnie. "It was drizzling and bitterly cold. I had been ordered to sit outside in the rain on the boat because I was not allowed to mix with the passengers inside. As I stepped on shore, cold, upset and depressed, I simply ignored the voice calling for my address. I had already signed the book with my name and address at the police station as I was required to do when reaching Cape Town, and I had handed in my permit as ordered, so I did not think it would be a policeman calling to me."

But it was and after appearing in court many times Winnie was found guilty of failing to give her name and address to the police. All but four days of the sentence were suspended. "As though they didn't know my address, watching me as they do all the time."

In spite of her own troubles she was involved in many activities to help others—particularly those connected with the banned ANC. Hearing that there was a large number of political prisoners in Nylstroom prison, most of them from Port Elizabeth, 700 miles away, Winnie managed to find out their names. Then she devised a way of cheering them. She knew full well the fears of imprisoned people who had no way of contacting the families left behind when they were arrested and she heard, too, that few of the Nylstroom prisoners ever received any mail.

Only relatives were allowed to send letters to political prisoners so Winnie enlisted the help of a group of Soweto women, each of whom was to write to a prisoner, pretending to be a relative. Helen Joseph, who was then working at the Anglican Cathedral in Johannesburg, was able to obtain funds so that a postal order could be enclosed with each letter. Another person who offered to help was Maude Katzellenbogen. When

111

later the police made arrests and it came out that they knew of these activities and of the leaflets printed at Maude's house and the cover addresses Winnie had used, Maude was the one person not charged.

Winnie became so inured to arrest that she prepared a small suitcase ready packed with necessities for a sojourn in jail and kept it at the front door of her house for easy access whenever she was taken away. Her daughters remember their bewilderment in their early years at having policemen constantly around the house and going through their mother's possessions. "I was quite young when I realized we were different but I did not know why," says Zeni. Her little sister, Zinzi, was stricken with fear every time she saw her mother taken away. She grew up, she says, always expecting to hear the loud banging on the door in the middle of the night.

Fortunately for the girls, they were extremely happy at Waterford, but dread of what might be happening to their mother was always with them. Zinzi, who learnt to play the piano and the guitar at Waterford, began composing her own music and expressing her feelings in verse. A collection was published in book form by Random House when she was in her mid-teens, and something of her agony is revealed in this verse:

> I need a neighbour who will live
> A teardrop away
> Who will open up when I knock late at night
> I need a child who will play
> A smile away
> Who will always whisper I love you
> To be my mummy.

The two children were home for the holidays and in bed on 12 May 1969 when Winnie was awakened at two in the morning by a police raid. They stormed into the house, lifted her daughters, then aged nine and ten, from their beds to search beneath the bedclothes, and stripped the house of documents, even taking the books that Nelson had acquired during his student days. They removed his typewriter and confiscated the clothing he wore at his first and second trials. Then, their search concluded, they told Winnie she was being detained. Indefinite detention without trial is legal in South Africa and scores have disappeared into oblivion under those regulations. There was no one with whom to leave Zeni and Zinzi so the police drove the two girls in the middle of the

112

night to the home of one of Winnie's sisters, seven kilometres away. It was the last time the children were to see their mother for a year and a half.

Winnie had dropped out of the world. Only from her distraught daughters did her relatives and friends realize that she had been detained.

Chapter Ten

WHEN SHE WAS whisked away that May morning Winnie realized that this was no ordinary arrest. She was refused permission to contact her lawyer, relatives, friends or a minister of religion. News of her absence travelled fast. Nelson tried in vain through his lawyers to find out where his wife was being held and why. All inquiries met with a wall of silence about Winnie's detention under the laws that allowed her to be held incommunicado indefinitely.

She was one of several people detained that day but it was only much later that she discovered others had been picked up at the same time. She was taken to Pretoria Prison and when the door of her tiny cell clanged shut she believed she was alone in her misery.

For the next 491 days—seventeen months—she was to endure extreme emotional and psychological torture, most of it in solitary confinement under the grimmest conditions imaginable. For the first 200 days she had no contact with anyone outside. A coir mat on the floor of her cell was her bed; two filthy urine-stained blankets her sole protection against the biting cold of the Transvaal winter. The only other items in her cell were a plastic litre bottle of water, a mug and a home-made sanitary bucket without a handle. Winnie, whose phobia for cleanliness has always amused her family, was utterly revolted by that object. As well as using it as a lavatory she had to wash in it by pouring some of the precious water from her one-litre bottle on to her hands over the bucket.

At mealtimes her food plate was placed on top of the sanitary bucket which was removed once a day for emptying but was often returned only partly cleaned. The cell stank. It had two grilles and three locks which had to be opened with three different sets of keys before the white wardress could enter. "It was shattering to wait for those three sets of locks to be undone. It was the sort of psychological torture you never forget," recalls Winnie.

Breakfast consisted of under-cooked porridge without sugar or milk. Lunch was whole mealies and for supper there was porridge again, sometimes with a little spinach added. The spinach, slimy and gritty, was scarcely edible and had clearly been put straight into the pot from the soil without being washed. Once a week, on Sundays, a small piece of tough, fatty pork was added. To drink there was either black coffee without sugar or a mealie meal drink served in clay pots. When Winnie was finally released her smooth skin was blotched with the unmistakable signs of the prolonged lack of vitamins in her diet.

Week after week, month after month, she languished in her cold concrete cell. The light was kept on day and night. There was no one to speak to and nothing to read or do. To keep her sanity she tore one of her blankets into pieces, thread by thread, and then wove the threads together, just as, in her childhood, she had watched her grandmother doing when making traditional mats with a grass called uluzi. Her desperation was such that often she would scour the tiny cell to see if she could find an ant or a fly. "You cannot imagine the joy there was in seeing a living creature," she recalls.

Although she scratched dates on her cell wall, the complete isolation and utter silence of her surroundings made it difficult for Winnie to keep track of time which could be measured only by the three meals taken to her cell each day. The only occasions on which she saw any other prisoners was at mealtimes. The white wardress would kick open the door after the triple unlocking and a black prisoner would run in carrying Winnie's plate of food, put it down on top of the sanitary bucket and run out again, too scared even to glance Winnie's way.

Two weeks after her detention her interrogation began. By now she was such a well-known personality that the police did not dare mark her with physical torture such as was endured by lesser-known detainees, but they had other means of trying to break her spirit. For five days and five nights she was interrogated ceaselessly, standing all the time under a brilliant light. Teams of interrogators under Major J. Swanepoel, described by many prisoners as a skilled torturer, took it in relays to conduct the non-stop questioning. The mental torture of those days was acute. Winnie knew that everything depended on her staying sufficiently alert so as not to break down and incriminate her friends. To her dismay she soon discovered by their questions that the police knew all about her cover addresses, all about the pamphlets she had printed at Maude's house and all about the scheme to help the political prisoners in Nylstroom jail. Fortunately they were unaware of other activities.

"They bring you food during the questioning but something happens when you are being interrogated and even though your stomach is rent with hunger pains you cannot swallow food. I just drank water during those five days. My arms and legs swelled up like balloons and when they helped me to the lavatory I could scarcely put one foot in front of the other.

"Many times I fainted—it was nature's way of giving me relief when I could endure no more. But as soon as I came round I was put on my feet again and the interrogation went on. Major Swanepoel kept warning me not to die on him till I had given him the information he wanted.

"They asked me over and over again about political acts, saying I was responsible for inciting people. They claimed those arrested in acts of sabotage had taken their instructions from me which was absurd. Then they told me they had also detained an eighteen-year-old mother called Charlotte who had once stayed in my house with her baby. She was innocent of an involvement but they said that unless I made a statement they would keep her in prison indefinitely. They work on the theory that if you want to know what a banned person is up to, you detain and question other members of the household to make the banned person confess.

"On the fourth day of my continuous interrogation I started urinating blood, and my fainting fits became more frequent. I was nearly at the end of my tether. Finally, on the Saturday, I gave in. I said I would accept responsibility for everything if they would release the others. Everything they told me to admit I admitted." Back in her cell she slept, utterly exhausted.

Two months after her arrest Major Swanepoel walked into Winnie's cell and asked her who Thembi Mandela was. She replied that he was her stepson. Callously, Major Swanepoel told her: "Well, he is dead. He was killed in a car accident," and left the cell.

Winnie wept for the first time since her detention. Thembi was just nineteen and Nelson's much-loved elder son. She grieved not only for the boy but for the blow she knew it would be to Nelson. Later, when they were in contact again, she realized just how deeply the tragedy had affected him. Word of Thembi's death spread through the prison by bush telegraph and resulted in Winnie receiving her first inter-cell communication. Seldom can words of comfort have been received in such a strange way.

When Winnie's sanitary bucket was returned next day it had not been properly emptied. Being used to this partial cleansing of the pail she did

116

not take particular notice till later when her plate of food was brought in. As she lifted the plate from the top of the bucket she noticed a piece of silver paper protruding from the muck at the base. Never having had any silver paper in her cell Winnie removed it carefully and unwrapped it. Inside was a message sending her sympathy from the other prisoners on the death of her stepson and adding: "Mother of the Nation, we are with you." Winnie was only thirty-three, but already she was being venerated just as Nelson was. She had no pen or pencil to write back but she did have a pin and with this she pricked out a few words on the silver paper and replaced it in the pail. A means of communication with others had now been established.

The next message, wrapped in a banana skin at the bottom of the bucket, said: "Go carefully, Joyce is breaking down. They are arranging to take her to Nylstroom to testify against you." Joyce Sikakane, a young reporter on the *Rand Daily Mail* and a granddaughter of the late Revd A. M. Sikakane, a founder of the ANC in 1912, was another detainee who was being mercilessly interrogated in an effort to obtain evidence against Winnie. In a crafty move such as they sometimes employed the police had provided special privileges for Joyce, knowing that this would make her fellow prisoners believe she had "turned" when in fact she had not. With her pin Winnie pricked out on the banana skin the words: "Joyce, you dare." It was not much but whether because of that, or because she had never intended to, Joyce refused to testify.

Now Winnie learnt more of others who had been detained with her. The deathly silence she had endured for months was broken when a prisoner was moved into a nearby cell. Suddenly, to her joy, she heard a Xhosa voice raised in song. A young woman's voice began with the words "My name is Nondwe" and carried on to improvise in song an account of how she and others had been detained; how one of their number, Michael Shivute, had died suddenly on the night of his detention and another, Caleb Mayekiso, had died nineteen days afterwards. Another of their number, Rita Ndzanga, a fellow activist and close friend of Winnie's, had had to leave her four small children at home when she was arrested, then she had been badly tortured and news had come to her in jail of her husband's death while he, too, was in prison. Saddened as she was by the news in that song Winnie now knew she was not alone.

Meanwhile, Nelson's frantic efforts to get information about his wife having failed, his legal representatives applied to the Supreme Court for an order directing that the detainees be given basic facilities. The application was granted and as a result Winnie was given the chance to wash properly. She had been 200 days without a bath or a shower and with only a litre of water a day to use for drinking and for all her ablutions. The most unforgettable moment of her isolation was when she received something to read. It was a bible. "It gave me a wonderful feeling of floating, as if I had taken a drug," recalls Winnie.

"Major Swanepoel came to my cell with the bible. He was flanked by officers, all in uniforms with shiny buttons. It seemed to give them a sadistic satisfaction to stand there looking so imposing. Swanepoel flung a bible right to the back of my cell telling me: 'There, pray to your God to have you released from detention. But you will pray in Xhosa, not in English!'

"They had a thing about my speaking English and not Afrikaans which I refuse to speak as it is the language of my oppressor. As their English is not good sometimes we could not understand each other. When this happened Swanepoel would rage like a mad animal. I really believe that the basis of some of the greatest friction and animosity in this country is caused by people of different races not understanding each other's language. The Afrikaner is obsessed with this raw unknown language of his. It is his identity and if you do not speak it he thinks you are rejecting his authority. That is partly why so many had to die in Soweto," says Winnie, referring to the riots of 1976.

Five months after they had been arrested the detainees—19 of the original 22 held—were due to appear in court for the first time. Major Swanepoel insisted on Winnie (who still had no access to anyone outside) signing a power of attorney authorizing a lawyer named Mendil Levin to act for her. This was in spite of the fact that he knew Nelson had sent word that he wished Joel Carlson to appear for his wife. Then, after telling Winnie she must advise the other detainees to engage Levin to represent them too, Swanepoel took them to her one by one. Winnie seemingly did as she was told, telling them in Xhosa what Swanepoel said, but each time slipping in an extra sentence saying, "This Levin is a police lawyer. Do not employ him." They understood.

On the day the detainees were due to be charged Swanepoel and Levin arrived in the courtroom confident that Levin would be representing all the accused and that the case would be disposed of quickly. But Joel Carlson, a well-known Johannesburg political lawyer, was there, too, to tell the judge that Winnie's husband had engaged him to defend her but that he had been denied access both to his client and to the other accused whose relatives also wanted him to appear for them. The judge ordered that Carlson be given a chance to speak to the detainees and when the court re-assembled it was to hear that all the accused had denied wanting to be represented by Levin. He then had to retire from the case while an embarrassed Swanepoel looked on, powerless to intervene, as Joel Carlson took over.

The trial was held before a judge and assessors. There were 21 charges with hundreds of sub-sections against Winnie, maintaining, among other things, that she had been receiving instructions from her husband on Robben Island and that she had revived the African National Congress. The evidence, however, was unbelievably flimsy. The prosecutor told the court he had 80 witnesses but they all turned out to be either police or detainees themselves, one of them Winnie's youngest sister, Nonyaniso. She told the judge she had been threatened with ten years in jail if she did not testify against Winnie but that she had been harried so much she could no longer distinguish between what she knew and what the police had told her to say.

Several of the witnesses described how they had been tortured in an attempt to force them to give evidence against Winnie. Another witness, Shanti Naidoo, whose brother, Idris, was on Robben Island with Nelson, was sent to jail for two months for refusing to give evidence against her friends. She had already been detained for months in solitary confinement and she, too, had been kept standing for days while being interrogated. After 20 witnesses had given evidence the case was adjourned for two months, the detainees being taken back to their cells for that period. Then, when the case resumed on 16 February 1970, the Attorney General appeared in court to tell the judge that the state was abandoning its prosecution. Counsel and prisoners alike were amazed at this unexpected development. They listened, incredulous, as Mr Justice Bekker said:

"I find you not guilty and you are discharged." But, no sooner had the bemused detainees realized they were free than they were surrounded by police; they heard orders barked through a loud-hailer for the public to leave the courtroom and they watched, dismayed and apprehensive, as the police, armed with sub-machine guns, jostled the crowd through the doors, preventing them from approaching the detainees. Then all the accused were immediately re-arrested on the orders of General van den Berg, the ruthless head of the Bureau for State Security. They were taken back to their cells to be detained again in the same solitary confinement that had begun nine months before.

This move caused an outcry, but the implacable government ignored all criticism.

Then fifteen relatives applied to the court for an order restraining the police from torturing the detainees. While in contact with their lawyers during the period of the trial, the detainees had described their individual experiences at the hands of the torturers. Their sworn affidavits were submitted to the court but the judge was unmoved. He ruled that the matter was not urgent and when eventually it came up again he refused to make an order for the relief sought, dismissing the application with costs. Finally, in September 1970, Winnie and the others were charged again. Their counsel pointed out to the judge that of the 540 allegations in the new indictment, 528 were identical to those at the first trial, only individual words being altered here and there to suggest a difference.

For three days their counsel painstakingly read out, word for word, all the hundreds of allegations from both trials, pointing out how each one approximated the previous charge until the judge could bear no more and stopped him. Then the judge dramatically announced that the accused were acquitted for the second time and could go. Even their lawyers were stunned at the suddenness of the acquittal.

Winnie's 491 days cut off from the world were over, and nothing had been proved against her to justify them. But so inured was she to solitary confinement, and so dazed by her long incarceration, that after the acquittal she turned like a zombie to go back to her cell. Her lawyer had to take her arm and lead her out of the dock to her first taste of freedom in a year and a half. Outside there was pandemonium among the hundreds of relatives and sympathizers milling about, laughing, crying for joy and shouting excitedly, still scarcely believing that the long ordeal was over. Even the police, brandishing sten guns and yelling at the crowds to break up this illegal gathering, could not dampen their spirits.

Adjusting to normal life after seventeen months alone in captivity was a frightening experience. Winnie was completely disorientated at first, almost in a daze. She had to convince herself that she would no longer have to go back to her solitary existence, no longer have to endure that awful prison smell and the indignities and loneliness of cell life. She walked hesitantly out into the open air, bemused and only partly comprehending the congratulations being showered upon her. Her one coherent thought was that she must send telegrams to Nelson on Robben Island and to the children at school in Swaziland to tell them of her release.

Years later, on reading Gordon Winter's book, *Inside BOSS*, she learnt that the government had been so anxious to convict her that they had been willing to break Winter's cover and bring him back to South Africa from England to testify against her. However, neither he nor Maude Katzellenbogen, both of whom knew probably more than any of the other witnesses that time, was called to give evidence.

Many people coming out of detention were permanently scarred mentally by their experiences and Winnie's friends had feared for the effect her horrendous treatment might have had on her. But the buoyant and indomitable spirit that had kept her going through all her troubles in the past was as strong as ever, and her friends marvelled to see how quickly she took up the threads of life once more.

Her banning order had expired while she was in prison and it was two weeks before the police got round to re-imposing it. In the meantime she had a fortnight of freedom after seven years of continuous banning. She took advantage of the opportunity to go to the Transkei to see her father.

It was many years since they had seen each other and both were relieved at having the opportunity to heal the rift that had parted them for so long—not only in person but in spirit, too. Columbus, now a much respected seventy-year-old member of the Transkei cabinet formed in anticipation of independence, was, like his colleagues, living in a palatial house in Umtata, but he was failing in health and troubled by misgivings about the benefits of the coming "independence". It was a happy reunion, though Winnie was saddened to see how her father had aged, while Columbus was concerned at the haggard appearance of his beautiful daughter.

He confided to Winnie that she had been right after all—he was having grave doubts about the wisdom of establishing the Transkei as an "independent" state. No longer did he believe this would be the answer to the injustices suffered by blacks. He had been misguided in thinking things would change. Poverty, overcrowding and unemployment were worsening, he told her. Every week the South African government was endorsing out thousands of blacks from the urban areas and dumping them in the Transkei without jobs or money. Worst of all, the pernicious migrant labour system had been intensified. The idea of "independence", he now saw, was nothing less than a ruse to justify the denial of political rights to black South Africans.

The reunion and reconciliation with her father cheered Winnie enormously. The return to her roots did much to restore her balance and back in Soweto she felt refreshed and more determined than ever not to be diverted from her purpose in life.

As soon as Winnie had been released from detention her lawyer had applied for permission for her to visit her husband. On her return from the Transkei she was told the application had been refused. Outwardly she raged at such inhumanity. Inwardly she wept, near to despair. There was another blow, too. On 30 September 1970 she was placed under house arrest, forbidden to leave her home between 6 p.m. and 6 a.m. or at weekends. And, far from leaving her alone now that she had been acquitted, the security police harassed her more than ever to the extent that her attorney asked the court to restrain them from visiting her so frequently. At times, he said, police arrived at her house four times a day. She had no privacy.

The public at large knew very little about the conditions under which Winnie had been detained—the Prisons Act prevented newspapers from publishing anything about penal institutions. However, reports of her two trials and two acquittals, followed by her house arrest and the refusal to allow her to see Nelson, gave some indication of the vendetta against her. There was a storm of protest from some religious and political leaders at the refusal to allow her to visit her husband. It was dubbed inhuman, unbelievable and ridiculous.

A month later Winnie made another application to visit Nelson. Because of the furore the previous refusal had aroused, the then Minister of Justice, Mr P. C. Pelser, announced that he would handle the application himself. This time it was granted.

The very next day Winnie flew to Cape Town and took the ferry to Robben Island to see Nelson for the first time in two years. It was a traumatic meeting. All she wanted to do was to rush into his arms but she was not even allowed to touch his hand. To be so close and yet so distant gave her a feeling of intense frustration. The warders stood close, listening for any innuendo, and in the background she could hear the whirr of the tape-recorder. She could see Nelson only from the waist up through glass and the time sped by before either of them managed to express adequately to the other their true feelings. It was the first time she had been able to commiserate with Nelson, too, on his son's death.

To have to leave again after only 30 minutes was harder than she would have believed possible. She stumbled back to the ferry, to the airport and back to Johannesburg. When she reached her home in Soweto all the strains of her long incarceration, coupled with the excitement of seeing Nelson, seemed to crowd in on her. She had a heart attack. She was only thirty-four. The enforced rest gave her a breathing space to revitalize her flagging spirits.

After her release from detention the security police, frustrated just when they believed they had succeeded in putting her away for a long time, renewed their "dirty tricks" against her. She discovered the first evidence of this when she returned from visiting her father to find her home had been ransacked. She set about restoring to the shelves the books that had been left lying on the floor, and as she picked up her large Xhosa bible it fell open revealing that the pages had been expertly hollowed out to form the shape of a gun. She knew it was meant to intimidate her so she said nothing to the police. But she showed it to her friends and kept it for years till it disappeared mysteriously when the police packed her belongings six years later.

During the next three years repeated efforts were made to try to obtain convictions against Winnie. Some of the charges she faced could only be described as absurd. There was the time, for instance, when she was charged with receiving more than one caller at a time. These included a toddler and a nine-month-old baby, members of her family brought on a visit by relatives. Another time, after her front door had been broken down by a man claiming to be from the security police, three white sympathizers who had read of the attacks on Winnie called at her home with the loan of a guard dog for her protection. They were arrested, charged and fined for visiting a banned person and Winnie was charged with allowing them to visit her with a dog!

A friend of Winnie's, Angela Cobbett, a leading member of a white liberal women's organization known as the Black Sash, was arrested for taking her the gift of an Alsatian to replace the guide dog that had only been loaned to her. The dog, Sheba, was killed mysteriously with poisoned meat not long afterwards.

There was a whole series of attacks during 1972. Her friends engaged a watchman to protect her house but he was unable to prevent three men, two white and one black, from bursting into Winnie's home when she was absent. When he protested they showed him their police identity cards and searched the place thoroughly. In daylight next morning the watchman found that all the clothing on the line, including one of Winnie's dresses, had been slashed with a knife. Later that year her car was stolen. Then a man wielding a knife was caught by neighbours outside her home, and soon afterwards came the most frightening attack of all.

Winnie was asleep one night with her ten-year-old niece beside her. The child was staying with her for company, children being exempt from the ban on contact with Winnie at night. Being a light sleeper, Winnie was instantly awake when she heard a noise in her bedroom. Quietly she reached out to the bedside lamp and switched it on to reveal three men in the room. One was holding a wire noose in his hand as he advanced towards the bed.

"I was determined that if I had to die I was going to put up a fight and take one of them with me," says Winnie. She sprang out of bed but a fight was averted by the piercing shrieks of her niece, loud enough to wake all the neighbours. The men turned and fled.

Winnie phoned her lawyer and her vigilante friends, who discovered that the burglar bars on one of her windows had been sawn right through and then carefully replaced. They insisted she phone the police which she did, though she knew it would be useless. "They took a statement and that was the end of the matter," says Winnie. "It is quite extraordinary how efficient the police are when they are investigating other crimes, but no culprit has ever been brought to account for any of the offences against me or my property—bombing, housebreaking, attempts at shooting, strangling and stabbing me, damage to my house and possessions—all these have baffled the police. It is very strange that not one of the perpetrators of those crimes has ever been traced."

When a bomb exploded against the side of her house Winnie had no doubt as to its origin. "No black man throws a bomb at the house of Nelson Mandela," she asserts with conviction.

Her younger daughter, Zinzi, then only twelve but wise to the vendetta being waged against her mother and horrified at the violence and frequency of the attacks, wrote to the United Nations appealing to them to protect her mother. In response the Secretary General of the UN and the International Red Cross both asked the South African government for assurances about Winnie's safety. In the light of this appeal from influential overseas sources Winnie felt more confident that there would be no fatal attack on her now. Nevertheless, her friends came up with a scheme to protect her by building a wall right round her corner house. Two members of the vigilante committee involved in the wall operation were Horst Kleinschmidt, a member of the Christian Institute, and Father Cosmos Desmond, a Franciscan priest who wrote *The Discarded People* about the victims of the government's resettlement scheme for blacks. He was banned and house arrested in South Africa, later renouncing his calling and returning to London. The wall generated a great deal of amusement in the coming months as it was so fraught with obstacles, one upon the other.

Horst Kleinschmidt (who is now the Director of International Defence and Aid in London) was overseeing the operation. One of the last things Nelson had done before his imprisonment was to plant an evergreen hedge around his house, but with Winnie so often absent in detention the hedge had died through lack of water. However, the stumps were still there and Horst instructed the builders to use them as a guideline for the erection of a vibracrete wall. It was well under construction when the authorities complained that the line of demarcation was wrong as it encroached on the boundary of a neighbouring plot. Nelson had planted the hedge askew! The wall had to be pulled down and a new boundary marked out. At the second attempt the builder went bankrupt halfway through the job. So another firm was engaged, but this time when Winnie saw the completed section she pointed out that it was far too low for safety as anyone could step over it. The committee agreed, but now all the supporting posts had to be ripped out of the concrete in which they were embedded and taller posts erected. More money had to be raised for the higher wall to be built. Eventually it was completed around the four sides of the plot but even then it was not absolutely secure, for there were gaps for entry. Nevertheless the saga of its erection had produced as much frivolity as frustration and cemented a number of friendships.

The attacks on Winnie paled into insignificance when news came in September 1973 that her father was dying. She sought—and was granted—permission to go to the Transkei to see him. Taking her children with her she sped to his bedside.

Although by then Columbus was too weak to walk and could barely stand, he insisted that Hilda, his wife, should dress him in his best suit, unaware that it now hung baggily on his shrunken frame, and then support him so that he could stand upright to meet his visiting family. Even on his deathbed the aura of the schoolmaster did not leave him.

"My daughter and grandchildren," he said, standing erect with difficulty, "I want you to remember me like this." Winnie kissed him for the first and only time in her life. He had been her inspiration and the rock on which she had leant throughout her childhood.

In spite of their differences over the Bantustan (homeland) issue, she remembers him as a "wonderful, unforgettable character, imbued with compassion for his own people so unjustly treated and determined that the younger people should right the wrongs." She was thankful that in spite of their isolated quarrel her father, before he died, had understood her motives in becoming a political figure to fight for a free South Africa.

Some months after her father's death Winnie went to prison following one of her rare convictions. The case had been hanging fire for a long time pending appeal. Originally she had been sentenced in the lower court to twelve months' imprisonment on a charge that many considered trivial.

The incident that landed her in court occurred in full public view in broad daylight with no prior arrangement. In her lunch hour she had met her children who were home from boarding school. On her way back to her office it began to rain heavily. As the trio stood on a street corner waiting to cross the road they spotted Peter Magubane in his kombi at the traffic lights. The children cried out: "There's Uncle Peter," and Winnie called to him across the street: "Can you give these two a lift home?" He assented, so Winnie, holding the children's hands, took them over to the kombi and was promptly arrested and charged with talking to another banned person. Magubane suffered the same fate.

Her daughters were in court when they heard their mother sentenced to twelve months in jail for, as it seemed to them, seeking to get them a lift home in the rain. Zinzi burst into tears. Winnie's lawyer gave notice of appeal and Cosmos Desmond provided bail so she could be released in the meantime. As soon as the court rose Winnie, normally the most indulgent of parents, turned furiously on Zinzi.

"You will *never* cry in front of a white policeman again!" she admonished. It was a lesson the little girl never forgot and one that helped her to face the persecution that has followed her, too, into adulthood, and to display the same stoicism as her mother.

In September, 1974, when the appeal was heard, the sentence was reduced to six months' imprisonment. Prepared on this occasion, Winnie had arranged for her girls, who were home again from boarding school, to stay at their house in Orlando under the watchful eye of a tribal elder who lived nearby, while Horst Kleinschmidt was given the task of taking care of the financial arrangements. Their guardian, Dr Motlana, was also

Winnie Mandela

at hand to help and many other friends offered their support, so this time Winnie felt easier about the parting.

For the first month of her sentence she was held at the Johannesburg Fort. Then one midnight (presumably to avoid being seen by sympathizers) she was transferred to the vast Kroonstad Prison where she served the remainder of her sentence. That incarceration was a huge improvement on the horrendous conditions she had suffered during her seventeen months of solitary confinement in Pretoria. Nevertheless, the claustrophobic effect of those grey, uncommunicative walls drove her to a state of desperation, she recalls. But it was a relief—and an inspiration—to find she was to share her confinement with two other political prisoners. The three of them were held in a special self-contained section of the prison—well away from the other inmates. They each had a tiny cell with the luxury of a communal bathroom and a tiny exercise yard surrounded by a high wall obscuring all but the sky.

Winnie's two companions in this prison within a prison were both remarkable women as dedicated to the cause as she was. One of them was Dorothy Nyembe who devoted her life to fighting for justice and who was doing fifteen years for harbouring guerrillas, making her the longest-serving woman political prisoner in the country. (She was released in April 1984, after serving the full sentence handed down in 1969—there being no remission for political prisoners.)

When Winnie joined her in Kroonstad Prison Dorothy had been in jail for five years. "I was shocked to see how the years of suffering and sacrifice showed on Dorothy," recalls Winnie. "She was a devout Christian and committed fighter for the freedom of our people. Even after all the hardship she had endured her devotion to the people and the cause was still uppermost in her mind. And her lack of bitterness in situations where others would have raged is a quality in her I will always envy." Even when Dorothy described how Gatsha Buthelezi (Chief Minister of the Kwazulu Bantustan in Northern Natal) had testified against her she was extremely understanding and conciliatory—something that Winnie says she finds impossible to emulate as, to her, Buthelezi remains "a political prostitute".

The third woman in the trio was Amina Desai, whom Winnie describes as being a remarkable woman of tremendous strength and upright character. Amina had been involved in the Timol case. Ahmed Timol, a thirty-year-old Indian schoolteacher, was said by the police to have dived out of an upper-storey window while being interrogated. But, according

127

to the inside information of Gordon Winter, who describes the event in his book, two security policemen had been holding Timol out of the window upside down, threatening to drop him if he did not stop telling lies. Then something happened to cause one of them to let go by mistake, and Timol crashed to his death ten floors down on the pavement below.

Amina Desai proved a wonderful source of inspiration to Winnie and the two remained firm friends after their release. Even today Amina regularly sends Winnie gifts of clothing and shoes knowing that she is prevented from working for a living and is entirely dependent on the charity of friends, known and unknown.

Time dragged for Winnie in Kroonstad in spite of the common cause she found with the other two political prisoners. She was allowed to sew and to read for there was a library at the jail but books had to be taken out for them by the white wardress who chose only "trashy" novels. Winnie's relationship with the dim-witted Afrikaner jailers was extremely tense. She found that the head wardress, Erica van Zyl, who had a degree in penology, was the only one "with anything between her ears". This woman, realizing that the prisoners were accustomed to a reasonable standard of living and were entitled to a modicum of personal respect, provided them with new blankets and unused prison uniforms.

When she returned to Johannesburg after serving her sentence Winnie obtained the first really well-paid post she had held since leaving the Child Welfare Society. She was employed at a firm called Frank and Hirsch at a salary of R250 a month. Her employer refused to be intimidated by the police or to accede to their suggestion that she should be dismissed. He told them it was the policy of his company to employ only people who were capable and worthy of their jobs, no matter whether they were black or white, and Mrs Mandela was an expert at her work.

In October 1975, when Winnie's third banning and house arrest order expired, she was told they would not be renewed. For ten months she was able to mix with other people, go where she wished and address meetings, though she said at the time: "I am not free. There is no such thing as freedom for me and my people yet. If anything my banning has made me more determined than ever to see change."

During this brief period of "freedom" Winnie travelled to Durban to address a reception given by Mrs Fatima Meer, an Indian sociologist on the staff of the University of Natal. Mrs Meer had played a leading role in anti-apartheid activities in Natal and had suffered long periods of banning which restricted her speeches and writing. She and Winnie had been closely associated in the Federation of South African Women and had formed the Black Women's Federation (later banned). More than 1,000 people of all races attended the reception in Durban, renewing their support for the fight against apartheid. It was a daunting experience for Winnie to be making a speech again after so many years of enforced silence. She had to constrain herself to speak in public and she did so on every possible occasion to get back into the way of it, so that it was not long before she had recovered her confidence.

Chapter Eleven

IN 1975 THE face of Southern Africa underwent a dramatic change. After protracted guerrilla wars in both Angola and Mozambique, the Portuguese finally withdrew and independence was established. Now only South Africa, Namibia and Rhodesia remained under minority rule. The black majorities in those countries drew enormous encouragement from the developments in the former Portuguese colonies. This was heightened in South Africa when South African troops, which had invaded Angola in support of Unita's Jonas Savimbi, had to retreat.

A growing mood of militancy and black consciousness was sweeping through black schools and colleges in South Africa. While the government was preoccupied with events to the north, a new phenomenon was arising on its own doorstep—schoolchildren in Soweto were rebelling.

The Bantu Education Act (education for servitude, the blacks called it), which had been introduced as part of the grand strategy of apartheid, had been in operation for two decades. It was a system detested and fiercely resented by the youngsters. Living in an urban environment with access to newspapers and the radio, they were well aware of the limitations their curriculum imposed on their advancement and were determined to do something about it.

They all seemed to know that Dr Hendrik Verwoerd (former Prime Minister and architect of Bantu education, who had been stabbed to death in the House of Assembly by an insane parliamentary messenger in 1966) had said: "There is no place for the Bantu in the European community above the level of certain forms of labour . . . Natives will be taught from childhood that equality with Europeans is not for them. People who believe in equality are not desirable teachers for Natives."

The dissatisfaction with the standard of their schooling was intensified among the children when a regulation was introduced forcing them to learn some of their subjects through the medium of Afrikaans instead of

English. They knew that this would limit their capabilities even further and they resented this imposition of a symbol of their oppression, as they regarded the Afrikaans language. Anger at the new measure united them in a mass show of solidarity that was to astound not only the authorities but even their own parents.

Winnie, freed for the first time from the restraints of a banning order, was back in the swing of things in Soweto and mixing freely among the people. She had a number of children staying at her home and was well aware of the growing anger among youngsters. Like many other prominent Sowetans she voiced her concern to the authorities at the introduction of such a provocative measure, warning that an explosive situation was developing and appealing to them to withdraw the ruling on instruction in the hated Boer language. Warnings and appeals were ignored.

Droves of anxious parents began calling on Winnie for advice as to how to respond to the way their children were rebelling. Some as young as eight years old were staying away from their lessons to protest. Most of the mothers were domestic workers who had had little or no education themselves. They were resigned to passive acceptance of the unfair system but they were determined their children should have a better deal in life and distressed that by staying away from school the pupils were jeopardizing their futures and the chance to be educated—even though that education was so restricted. Winnie heard an oft-repeated cry among the children that their parents had lain down under the heel of the white man for too long, and now it was the turn of the younger generation to fight for their rights.

In addition to her identification with the banned—but popularly supported—African National Congress she was an executive member of the Federation of South African Women and since the expiry of her bannings she had been seen and heard a great deal in Soweto. The parents believed that if anyone could help them Winnie could. Yet the tale that galvanized her into action was not the familiar one of children refusing to attend their classes. It was the story told her by a group of distressed parents whose children had been killed in a bus crash when they were on a school outing to Swaziland. Though they had been in the care of the authorities at the time, compensation, even for funeral expenses, was refused. So the parents raised the money themselves to bring back home the bodies of their children. The funds collected were sent off but never arrived at their destination—disappeared en route, it was said—and they could get no response to their complaints. That injustice spurred Winnie to act. What was needed, she reasoned, was an organization to look after the interests of Soweto parents.

With the help of influential professional friends in the township the Soweto Parents Association was launched in May 1976. Dr Aaron Mthlare, a former ANC activist, was chairman and Dr Motlana was among those on the executive with Winnie. The formation of the SPA was viewed with disapproval by the authorities. Whenever Winnie addressed a meeting of parents to explain the aims of the new body, which she did frequently, the security police were there taking notes and keeping a watch on her.

Just a week after the launching of the SPA two security policemen arrived at the Naledi High School in Soweto where Winnie had addressed a parents' meeting the previous weekend. They wanted to arrest one of the student leaders, Enos Ngutshana. Pupils asked their headmaster to tell the policemen to leave the premises and make any arrests outside the school grounds, but the policemen refused. Enraged, the pupils set alight the police car and beat up the two security policemen. That event did not become public till much later, believed to have been suppressed because of the ignominy of the powerful police being beaten up by "a bunch of kids". But that incident was the beginning of troubles that were to set Soweto alight in the coming weeks in an outburst of anger and resentment that was to spread throughout South Africa.

Working secretly, but with amazing efficiency and without consulting their parents, the children, through the Soweto Students Representative Council (SSRC) organized a mass protest against Afrikaans. It was to be a peaceful demonstration at which they would wear their school uniforms to give the lie to government allegations that outside agitators were responsible for stirring up trouble. Placards bearing slogans against the use of Afrikaans were prepared. Routes were worked out so that each school could march separately before converging on the main body. Just in case the police got rough the student leaders asked the headmasters of primary schools to see that their pupils stayed at home that day. However, the younger pupils were determined not to be left out and on 16 June—the day fixed for the protest—they joined the vast throng of youngsters singing freedom songs, raising clenched fists in the black power salute and carrying banners reading "Away with Afrikaans", "We are not Boers" and other anti-Afrikaans slogans.

Like the majority of adults in Soweto Winnie knew the children were planning a mass demonstration for that day but she had been assured it was to be a peaceful protest and believed it would be just that. "Had any of us had even an inkling of how it would turn out not one of us would have gone to work that day," she says.

As it was, when she dressed for the office that frosty June morning Winnie had no presentiment of tragedy. A thick pall of smoke hung over Soweto, the result of the tens of thousands of coal and paraffin fires by which most Sowetans kept warm and cooked. But soon there was to be smoke of a different kind over the townships, fuelled by the blazing buildings that symbolized apartheid to the children, and there would be a big black cloud over the future of white South Africa.

Winnie was going about her work as usual when she received a frantic phone call at her office from one of the Soweto mothers. Almost incoherent, the distraught woman screamed down the phone: "Please come, the police have started *shooting* our children." Winnie was so shocked she forgot to ask permission to leave her work. Grabbing her handbag she just ran to her car and drove at breakneck speed to Orlando West where she knew the children had been due to congregate.

Meanwhile, with the incredible speed with which the bush telegraph operates, word of the police action spread throughout Johannesburg. Hordes of blacks left their jobs and rushed home to Soweto—in trains, in buses, in lorries, in taxis, any way they could. Those with cars stopped to pack in as many others as possible—knowing the desperation parents felt to get home. Dr Nthato Motlana was an eye-witness of what happened before Winnie arrived on the scene and one of the few adults to see things from the beginning.

"I was there from the outset," he says. "On the morning of 16 June I saw a stream of schoolchildren marching past my house in Dube between seven and eight a.m. I followed them to see where they were going which is how I saw the violence erupt. They had just reached the Orlando West school when the police tried to stop them marching any further. The children kept on walking so the police released dogs. I did not see the pupils set upon the dogs but I know they did because later I saw a dead police dog that had been burnt. Then the police panicked and fired into the mass of children.

"All day I worked removing bullets and pieces of metal from children's bodies. Many of them were afraid of being taken by ambulance to Baragwaneth Hospital for fear of being identified and arrested so their parents carried them to my consulting rooms instead. It was the same for all the doctors in Soweto—we were working non-stop on children wounded in the firing."

Far from stemming the unrest by the shootings, the police action seemed to set off a trail of destruction in a frenzied fury against apartheid. But it is the stark horror of that first day that Winnie will never forget.

"As I drove through Orlando it looked like a battlefield," she recalls. "Police on the site of the bridge had turned it into a virtual military zone. The sea of black faces facing me is hard to describe. There were thousands of them. Little Hector Petersen, the thirteen-year-old boy who was the first to be shot, had just been killed and his body taken away.

"I will never forget the bravery of those children. They were carrying dustbin lids to protect themselves and deflect the bullets as they faced the police guns. The police had dogs and tear gas and batons but they chose instead to use bullets against those unarmed kids. The saddest sight anyone can see is a dying child ripped by bullets.

"The atmosphere was absolutely electric as the mob moved on to the main road. There I saw what no parent would ever wish to see—such violence! Police brutality had unleashed such rage among the pupils. Stones were flying like hail, cars and property were smashed, destroyed, set on fire; eleven-year-olds were driving Putco [Public Utility Transport Corporation] buses which they had hi-jacked; teenagers were hauling out drivers from government cars, burning down bottle stores, smashing everything in sight.

"There was nothing anyone could do to stop the mob on the rampage once they had been roused.

"There was one incident that still brings tears to my eyes. A delivery driver, an elderly man, was trying to drive through the crowds to carry out his duty and deliver his goods when he was ordered by a group of children to stop and get out. Seeing they were just kids and obviously not realizing the seriousness of the situation, he took no notice. Suddenly bricks were flying through his windscreen. One hit him on the forehead. He was flung out of the van and fell on his back in the road. He lifted his arm and shouted 'Amandla' but it was too late—he died under a hail of stones. Every time I think of those days I still see the face of that man.

"You can't make a crowd like that understand once they have lost control. It is hard to forget the sight of police pulling a white corpse out of a dustbin while children stand around singing freedom songs. This is the reality of what apartheid has done to the black man. How can a black child know right from wrong when one father will be put in jail for a technical offence like not having a pass and another for a real crime like murder? How do you define a criminal element in black society when they are the victims of violence all the time? The black child has no definition of a criminal.

"There was never any planned violence by the children, just an innocent demonstration against Afrikaans, and the government reacted, as it always does, with violence.

"The government claimed parents and children were divided, but this was not so. The pupils' hysterical reaction to the police shootings filled their mothers with dread. But whereas before the shooting some of the parents were inclined to be censorious when their children stayed away from school, now, after the shootings, they were united with them against the viciousness of the police. When things got out of control the parents had no alternative but to unite with the children and then the police turned against the parents too. The whole student leadership was on the run, so we had to be clandestine in assisting the SSRC to operate.

"Tsietsi Mashinini, the leader of the pupils, was dubbed 'the little Mandela' and one paper even went so far as to insinuate that he looked like Mandela and could be one of his sons."

Mashinini was only president of the SSRC for five months before he fled South Africa with a price on his head. His successor, Khotso Seathlolo, was shot and wounded and escaped to Botswana. But before that time the youngsters leading the children exerted a remarkable influence. Dr Motlana who, like Winnie, lived among the rebellious pupils, still wonders what factor it was that caused such an outstanding group of young men to arise at that particular time and to respond as they did.

"What chemistry it was that made them possible I do not know, but Mashinini was a most charismatic leader and there were others, too," he says. "Those youngsters organized things in a quite fantastic manner after the violence began—telling their parents and the workers what to do throughout the weeks of unrest."

Dr Motlana recalls seeing a vanload of police taking potshots at a group of little children of about six years old playing at the roadside. He rushed off to complain to the brigadier in charge of the Soweto police. "What the hell do you think you are doing shooting at little children?" he demanded. But, says Dr Motlana, the brigadier was rude and abusive. He adds: "Of course, we had a particularly stupid Minister of Justice

[Kruger] who exacerbated the situation by his behaviour. A more perceptive man would have ensured that the police behaved differently and with more restraint. The police claimed that I incited the children."

They made the same claim about Winnie, saying that she was responsible for setting the whole country alight.

"How I wish I did have such powers," comments Winnie. "Those riots were simply an expression of black anger and they started among school kids innocently protesting against Afrikaans."

Normally Soweto at night was a city of darkness, only a small part being electrified, but now night was turned into day with the fires of fury. In the ensuing weeks of unrest more than 50 government buildings, many of them schools, and 67 beer halls and bottle stores were burnt to the ground. Shops, post offices, houses and vehicles by the hundred were damaged or destroyed. Beer halls and bottle stores were a particular target of the children—beer halls because the profits went to finance the hated Bantu Administration Board and bottle stores because the children were incensed that their fathers spent so much of their meagre wages on liquor. Illegal shebeens were targets, too, and the liquor poured out into the streets to add to the stagnant puddles in the alleys.

Winnie's shebeen tycoon friend, Elija Msibi, was not harmed. He was solidly behind the protesters. He had been approached by the police to work for them, thinking that a man of his wealth would be against the revolt, whereas he sympathized with it wholeheartedly. He asked the ANC leadership how he should treat the police approach. They told him to pretend to help the police using his illiteracy as an excuse for not handing on to them any vital information. He was to say the students spoke only in English which he did not understand. The ruse worked and Elija was able to glean a great deal of useful information to pass on to Winnie. In this way he helped many youngsters elude the clutches of the police in the nick of time—sometimes hiding them in his own house till they could get away.

Thousands of schoolchildren were on the run but there was a tremendous spirit of unity among parents and offspring alike. Winnie, in common with other prominent Sowetans, was kept busy in the ensuing weeks of chaos. She comforted bereaved parents, obtained donations of coffins, arranged funerals of the victims and dealt with offers of help that poured in. Taxi drivers transported people free of charge to the burials. It was a deeply distressing time and there seemed to be no end to the violence which had spread to nearby Alexandra Township and along the Reef.

At the end of the carnage in Soweto official figures put the dead at 600. Winnie (and many other independent assessments) insists it was well over 1,000 killed, mostly children, some under twelve years old, with more than 4,000 others wounded. In addition, thousands of children disappeared across the borders to safety while many others disappeared into police detention. Hundreds of parents never found out what had happened to their children.

Winnie learnt with growing concern how the violence was spreading to other cities in South Africa. She urged the Soweto Parents Association to join with other organizations nation-wide to form a national Black Parents Association to fight for their rights instead of simply leaving it to their children to do so. Addressing a meeting of the Soweto Parents Association she told them:

"Not one of the big cities in which we are living today was built without our labour, no railway line without our hands. The country is what it is because of us but now we are driven out of the cities. We carry passes, not to conform to anyone's concept, but because we cannot marry, rent houses, register births or take a job without passes. Blacks belong to South Africa and it is our right to seek jobs anywhere, but we cannot do so without permits. Our children are now fighting for us while we do nothing."

Soweto parents decided to merge with the newly formed Black Parents Association. The chairman was Dr Manus Buthelezi (a cousin but no admirer of Chief Gatsha Buthelezi) and Winnie, Dr Motlana and Dr Mathlare were leading figures in it. The BPA agreed to act as the mouthpiece of the students by passing on their grievances to the authorities. But its main functions were to provide medical, legal and financial help after the riots.

Not everyone in Soweto, however, supported the BPA. The government-sponsored Urban Bantu Councils were very hostile to the new organization which they regarded as a threat to their position. Their animosity turned to personal attacks on BPA members. Threats became so menacing that in mid-August Winnie and Dr Motlana made an urgent and successful application to the courts to restrain the Soweto Urban Bantu Council from interfering with their homes and the lives of themselves and their children. The court heard that at a meeting of the UBC one of the councillors, Lucas Shabanga, had urged that the houses of Mandela and Motlana should be attacked and that the children who tried to prevent workers going to their jobs should be killed. It was claimed in court that the government had given the UBC permission to set up a Home Guard to attack the homes of BPA members and had given them permission to carry weapons. The UBC, it was also said, held its own courts to try minor criminal cases along the lines of tribal courts and those found guilty were publicly flogged. Although these courts had no legal standing and were widely despised by the young people, the government did nothing to prohibit them.

The protest through the courts was pre-empted when Winnie, Dr Motlana, Dr Mathlare and others were arrested and disappeared into detention. When Zeni and Zinzi arrived home from boarding school it was to discover that their mother had been detained along with 50 others, to be held in solitary confinement under the Internal Security Act. Riots, strikes and school boycotts had spread to many areas of the land as Winnie had predicted. In Soweto the revelation at the court case to restrain the UBC had greatly discredited that organization and its councillors found it necessary to go into hiding. When Dr Motlana was released from detention he became chairman of a committee of ten prominent Sowetans formed to take control of affairs in Soweto. The Committee of Ten, as it is still known today, soon eclipsed the discredited Urban Bantu Council and remains the most influential body in Soweto.

Winnie was kept in detention until January 1977, when she was released but placed under house arrest—having spent the previous five months in jail without being charged with any offence. Meanwhile the government appointed the Judge President of the Transvaal, Mr Justice Cillie, as a one-man commission to inquire into the Soweto riots. He was to hear thousands of hours of evidence and conflicting viewpoints as to the underlying causes of the riots before publishing his report.

Winnie went back to work at Frank and Hirsch, where her job had been kept open for her, and tried to pick up the threads of her life again, her irrepressible spirit rising once more in spite of all the harassment she had suffered. Forbidden to see anyone between 6 p.m. and 6 a.m., she kept herself busy at night studying by correspondence.

Chapter Twelve

JUST FOUR MONTHS after her release from detention, and nearly a year after the start of the Soweto riots, on the night of 15 May, Winnie had been working late putting the finishing touches to an essay for her degree course. It was past midnight when she climbed into bed. Zinzi, home from school in Swaziland, had been asleep for hours but her mother had barely dropped off when they were both awakened by the now familiar bashing at the front door, torches flashing and shouts of "Open up".

Wearily Winnie climbed out of bed to see what the police wanted this time. "Put your clothes on and come," she was told. Winnie did so and as she stooped to pick up the suitcase of necessities she always kept ready packed at the front door, she was told to leave it as she would not be needing it. Mystified, she followed the policemen outside, shielding her eyes against the brilliant lights from what seemed like dozens of headlamps trained on the house. There were a number of trucks parked outside and some 30 security policemen in camouflage uniforms milling about. It was 2 a.m. and bitterly cold. Still half asleep and not, as yet, unduly alarmed, for arrests were now a commonplace in her life and frequently had no discernible cause, Winnie was driven to the Protea Police Station in Soweto. There she realized there was something different about this arrest. She was not put into a cell nor was she told she was being charged. The men on duty passed jeering taunts about what was in store for her, but after a while she was left alone, sitting on a hard bench. She was shivering, both with cold and with apprehension about this "different" arrest; but, inured to hardship, she was determined that no one should notice her concern. It was an effort at that time of the morning to adopt an air of indifference, but in a crisis Winnie always found hidden reserves on which to draw.

They kept her waiting for several hours till Brigadier Jan Visser, at that time a colonel and the station commander, strode in with the paper authorizing her banishment. Banished! To a distant part of the land! She had been tried by no judge or jury and there was no appeal against this

139

order. Her plight was even worse than that of the two million who had been removed forcibly from their homes to the governments's new Bantustans. At least they were together with their families and friends whereas she would be alone.

"Brandfort—where in the world is that?" she puzzled. Those who had been banished in the past had been exiled to places in which they had grown up or where they had once lived. Brandfort and the province of the Orange Free State in which it lies might well have been a foreign country to Winnie—just what the government intended it to be. Blacks in Brandfort did not even speak Winnie's Xhosa mother tongue so, it was reasoned, she would be unable to influence anyone in that area as she had succeeded in doing in Soweto.

Waiting there with the banishment order in her hand, trying to come to grips with this new development, Winnie was planning all she must do before she left. She was unaware that there were to be no goodbyes, no opportunity to pack or put things in order. It was left to Zinzi, who arrived later at the police station, to acquaint her mother of the vindictive way in which the order was to be carried out. She was to be whisked off to Brandfort immediately, straight from the police station.

Zinzi described to Winnie how the police had moved into the house, bundled up clothing and curtains, carried the furniture and furnishings out of the house and crammed everything into the waiting transport to be conveyed to Brandfort with Winnie. When the house was quite empty a policeman told teenage Zinzi she had the choice of staying in the empty house until she returned to school in Swaziland or accompanying her mother into exile. Unhesitatingly Zinzi chose to go with her mother. "It was an incredible sacrifice for her to make and such a traumatic experience for her after the sheltered background of Waterford School," says Winnie.

Addressing Winnie formally before she was taken away, Colonel Visser told her that the Minister of Police (at that time the much detested Jimmy Kruger, the man who said Steve Biko's brutal death at police hands had left him cold) had decided to allow her R100 (about £50) a month, and from that sum would be deducted rent for the house she would occupy in Brandfort. Winnie told him to keep the money. "I have nothing left but my pride and nothing will induce me to accept a penny from my oppressors, and certainly not to pay rent for the jail to which you are taking me." No one seems to know what has happened to the money allocated to Winnie seven years ago.

It was rage at that final insult from Kruger that kept Winnie going throughout the long, tiring journey from Johannesburg to the Orange Free State. Her thoughts were in turmoil as they drove away. Would she ever see her beloved Soweto again? How she would miss the teeming crowds, the humour, the spontaneity, the community spirit and the gaiety of the people there, their courage transcending the hopelessness of their lives. How would her friends know where she had gone?

But Winnie reckoned without the press. As soon as word of this latest move against Nelson Mandela's wife became known, reporters and photographers were racing to Brandfort to arrive close on the heels of the banished. That is how they were on hand to see the appalling state of the little house at which Winnie was dumped.

During that journey to Brandfort the reality of what was in store caused even Winnie to wilt with dread. The further they travelled from the brash, bustling city of Johannesburg the more uninspiring did the sparsely populated Free State appear. For miles on end not a living soul was to be seen—just the flat veld, dry, brown and harsh. Then came the town of Brandfort—a drab place typical of an Afrikaner country town: neat little houses for whites only; old-fashioned two-storey hotels (also for whites only); a street of small shops and a perpetual Sunday after-noon atmosphere of lethargy and inactivity. It was daunting; but worse was to come.

Beyond the white part of the town, at the entrance to Brandfort's black township that no white person may enter without first obtaining a permit to do so, was the township superintendent's office. The slum township has no official name but its inhabitants call it Phatakele meaning "handle with care". If there is one word to describe the place it is forlorn, though even that word fails to convey the air of utter hopelessness about it.

Entering the township Winnie noticed how the barren ground was strewn with litter from a giant refuse pit. She leant forward to see what was moving in the pit and wished she hadn't. Women and children were scavenging among the filthy trash, desperately seeking some scrap from the refuse of the whites to eat or to use. It was a grim introduction to the horrors of the ghetto that was to be her home for the foreseeable future. As they drove past the first of the derelict-looking shacks of the township Winnie grew still more despondent. They pulled up at a newly built little square box of a house: No. 802, an address that was to become known throughout the world. It was semi-detached, with a flat roof, unfenced, sitting in a sea of dust. To Winnie's astonishment a gang of convicts was shovelling earth out from the interior of the house to make it habitable for the new arrival!

She still bridles with indignation when she recalls the state of that dwelling in which she and Zinzi were dumped. The narrow kitchen door was the only way in or out of the house—there was no front or side door. The house consisted of a tiny kitchen with two pocket-sized rooms leading off it, one a living-room, the other a bedroom. There was no electricity, no sewerage, no running water, no covering on the bare earth floors and not even a shelf on which to place a utensil. A few yards from the back of the house was a narrow pit privy that was to serve as their only lavatory for years to come.

Winnie and Zinzi watched impassively as their furniture and belongings were unloaded. Then came a farcical interlude that made Winnie chuckle even in her depressed state. Each piece of furniture in turn was taken to the narrow kitchen door and manipulated frontways, sideways and upside down in an effort to force it through the opening, to no avail. They tried the lounge furniture, the dining table, the refrigerator, the stove and the beds but every single item was too wide to go through the narrow entrance. For Winnie and Zinzi it provided a few minutes of light relief on that ghastly day. They smiled as they saw how the men pushed and swore and finally gave up, leaving the furniture on the ground while they consulted their superiors. When they returned it was to reload everything and cart it away, leaving only bedding, bundles of clothing and small objects on the dirty ground inside. The furniture was taken to the nearby police station, unloaded and stored there for a year, Winnie's refrigerator being plugged in at the police station so that she could make use of it.

Her first night in Brandfort is one she will never forget. The only water was at a communal tap in the street, serving about 80 houses. She and Zinzi had to queue with a long line of curious but strangely silent township dwellers to draw water to wash. Then, too tired even to eat the packet of chips that was to be their supper, they slept huddled together in the dark on a bundle of clothing on the floor of the empty little dwelling.

Voices from the adjoining semi woke them next morning and in the daylight they could now see that the dividing wall between the two dwellings reached only three quarters of the way up, leaving a deep gap between the top of the wall and the ceiling so that each side could hear every move or utterance made by the other. "I performed," says Winnie whose temper can be quite formidable when roused.

"The man next door was a security policeman brought especially from Zastron to watch me, but no matter who he was I was not going to have him listening to my every movement, nor did I want to hear everything he said.

"In Brandfort they had never heard of a black woman making demands. I think it was because they were so surprised that they gave in to my complaints and bricked up the wall. I complained, too, about the lack of cooking facilities and after a week of living on fish and chips I was provided with a little coal stove. They told me I could keep food in my own refrigerator that was plugged in at the police station and Zinzi and I had to call there several times a day if we wanted anything."

Winnie's Johannesburg employers, Frank and Hirsch, sent her her salary for the month of May and, to her astonishment and gratitude, continued to pay her R250 a month for a whole year after her banishment. When the money came Winnie went into the town to buy two narrow single beds that could be manoeuvred through the narrow door, paraffin lamps to lighten the early darkness of the winter nights and some groceries.

Unbeknown to her, apartheid was carried to ridiculous lengths in the Afrikaner dorp of Brandfort. She learnt later that till her arrival blacks had had to queue at a side window of the shops, shout out their requirements, indicate yes or no when the goods were held up out of reach for their inspection and make their purchases without ever entering the store. A crowd of blacks who had been following Winnie's progress through the town with unconcealed curiosity looked aghast when she walked into the grocery shop through the front entrance to buy her provisions. They waited to watch her thrown out but to their amazement this did not happen though all the whites in the shop at the time walked out, scandalized. The assistant, who had dealt only with servile black customers through the window, was too amazed at the effrontery of this imperious new arrival to do anything but accept her money meekly.

The week before Winnie's arrival in Brandfort residents of the township had been called by the Bantu Authority to an important meeting. There it was explained to them that a dangerous woman named Mrs Mandela was coming to live in their midst and that they must have nothing to do with her. Accustomed to doing as they were told, none of the blacks greeted Winnie on her arrival. The police were convinced that the language barrier would prove an insuperable obstacle anyway, for Winnie was Xhosa-speaking and the township residents spoke Sotho or Tswana. They reckoned without Winnie's sagacity and determination. She realized at once that her first priority was to learn the language so she could communicate with her fellows and encourage them to do something about their downtrodden lives.

In those first days Winnie was immensely heartened when friends, known and unknown, travelled hundreds of miles to see her. Mrs Bunty Biggs, who came from Pietermaritzburg, was the first person to bring her food. Mrs Biggs proved a good friend and even when she returned to England she continued to write to Winnie. Winnie's minister called from Johannesburg; sympathizers she had never heard of arrived with gifts of food and money after learning that she had been deprived of the chance to work and was now living on charity. That first trickle of visitors, many of them strangers till then, gave her new heart. The trickle was to grow into a stream but the first friendly faces were the most treasured.

Any thought of feeling sorry for herself was dispelled when she saw how Brandfort blacks lived. She wrote to a friend:

In my childhood in the Transkei I lived among poverty; in my social work in Johannesburg I saw even worse poverty, but never in my life had I imagined conditions as grim as those in this Brandfort ghetto.

I know the security police devised this punishment to destroy me morally and spiritually. They hoped to leave me in complete shreds but seeing the conditions here has made me more determined than I have ever been in my life to show them that I will continue ministering to my people and helping them in every way I can. I did not know anyone could be subjected to such appalling conditions as here, and this only a few hours from Johannesburg which is surrounded by the richest gold mines in the world.

Life here is very sad. Not a weekend passes without the funeral of a baby who has died. The mothers cannot afford milk for their infants so they make a substitute by braising a little flour in a pot outside, adding cold water to make a paste and then straining it through a cloth to produce a smooth liquid. On such a diet the babies' tummies soon become distended, their hair turns a silky red, they die of malnutrition and we have another pathetic walk to the cemetery.

Those women lucky enough to get jobs as domestic servants in the white houses in Brandfort at an average wage of R20 (about £10) a month, are given a midday meal of mealie pap and gravy by their white Afrikaner madams. Sometimes the madam just pours a little cooking oil over the porridge instead of gravy. In the evenings you see those domestic workers walking home with this little plate of food balanced on their heads and when they get back to the township the whole family sits around and makes a meal of that pap and gravy which is a delicacy to them.

This is one part of the country that has taught me that an Afrikaner will never share with a black man as he has never regarded him as a human being. Blacks are just labour units to them. Those Afrikaners in their smart white houses have no conscience about this ghetto over the hill.

But one white Afrikaner in Brandfort was to prove Winnie wrong in her assessment that all the Afrikaners living there lacked interest in the blacks on their doorstep. She was Mrs Adele de Waal.

Mrs de Waal is the wife of Brandfort's only attorney, Piet de Waal. Winnie's attorney in Johannesburg, Ismail Ayob, had advised her to make herself known to an attorney in Brandfort who would then liaise with him in dealing with any matters affecting her. So, having discovered his name, Winnie walked into Mr de Waal's office saying she would like him to act for her. When she told him her name there was a stunned silence. Only the shaking of the paper he held in his hand told Winnie how shocked he was. Recovering, he broke the silence by asking her to wait for a few minutes as he had something to attend to first.

Some time later, when he and his wife, incredibly for Free State Afrikaners, had succumbed to Winnie's charm and become friends, Piet de Waal described to her what had happened during those few minutes he was away. He had rushed round to the police station for instructions on how he should treat the matter, explaining to the officer in charge that he could not refuse to take on a legitimate client who had been referred to him by another attorney. He was given permission to do his duty and since then he has acted for Winnie in countless matters that have required attention either in Brandfort or as go-between with Ismail Ayob in Johannesburg.

Mrs de Waal is typical of many South African whites who, while perhaps not imbued with the racial bigotry that is so much a part of that society, simply never have occasion to challenge their own attitudes and prejudices. It is to Winnie's credit that many white people meeting her are jolted into questioning that ingrained attitude of theirs without in any way feeling themselves threatened. Undoubtedly Mrs de Waal was one of those people. The irony of her friendship with Winnie is that Mrs de Waal was formerly Adele Retief, a descendant of Piet Retief, one of the revered Voortrekker leaders killed by the great Zulu king, Dingaan, when the Boers sought to obtain part of the Zulu lands for themselves.

In the face of ostracism from other whites in Brandfort for such outrageous behaviour, Adele de Waal became a friend to Winnie. "It was the first time a kaffir had sat down in her lounge," laughs Winnie. Mrs de Waal took her food, lent her books and allowed her to use her bathroom to take a proper bath, for without a sink or wash-basin in her home Winnie had to go through a tortuous procedure of collecting several buckets of water from the tap in the street, warming them on the stove and then filling a zinc tub which had to be lifted into the little kitchen. "It is just as well I learnt to carry a bucket of water on my head as a girl, because I had to go back and forth from that street tap countless times to collect enough water for washing and cooking before my own tap was installed," says Winnie. Mrs de Waal's offer of the use of her bathroom, therefore, was a practical help that was much appreciated. In return Winnie helped Afrikaans-speaking Mrs de Waal to become proficient in English, and no doubt proved by her manner, her bearing and her conversation, that she was not the ogre she had been painted by the government.

Another friend who proved his worth to Winnie over a long period is the Bishop of Pretoria, the Rt Revd John Rushton. Before his recent transfer to Pretoria he was Archdeacon of Bloemfontein during the first six years of Winnie's stay in Brandfort. For those six years he travelled from Bloemfontein to Brandfort every fortnight to conduct a communion service for Winnie in his car as she may not enter a church without permission. Winnie has consistently refused to seek that permission.

"They say I can go to church in spite of my banning order provided I make application to do so but I will not ask for permission to worship my God. That gives a human being a stature that does not belong to him. As it is I cannot attend any gathering of more than two people, I cannot enter any educational premises, I cannot look for jobs. I am confined to the house for twelve hours of the twenty-four and for the other twelve hours to the magisterial district of Brandfort. I live on charity. I have always worked to support my family and I had a future as a social worker. Now they have dumped me here and insulted me by offering me R100 a month. All I have left is my pride."

A friend who called to see Winnie in Brandfort just days after her banishment, asked a black petrol attendant the way to her home. The attendant's face showed consternation as he warned the visitor to keep away from Mrs Mandela as they had been told she was a dangerous terrorist. Three months later, when the same man returned to Brandfort, the petrol attendant, recognizing him, greeted him like a long-lost friend, smiling broadly and raising his fist in salute, calling out "Amandla" (freedom). Winnie had made yet another convert in the face of all the propaganda waged against her. In the course of a few brief months she succeeded in awakening a good many of Brandfort's black population, an astonishing feat given the extent of their previous subservience.

Today the black township is solidly behind her but it has been an uphill task. Only someone of Winnie's calibre could have surmounted the difficulties in her path and the efforts of the authorities to scare the townsfolk into shunning any association with her.

Raids on her home continued. She was under constant surveillance while letters to and from her failed to reach their destination. Her only contact with the outside world was the public telephone at the post office in the white town. Winnie arranged with her friends to phone her there at 11 a.m. and 4 p.m. each day and twice daily she would make the long trek to the post office to sit and wait for the telephone to ring.

Winnie's arrival in Brandfort had been causing upheaval for blacks and whites alike. After her first sally through the white entrance of the shops one or two blacks tentatively followed suit. When nothing happened to them after Winnie had created a precedent, others did the same. A long-standing taboo had been ended but not without complaint. Afrikaners in the town gave interviews to the Sunday newspapers, bitterly condemning the arrival of Mrs Mandela who, they said, was corrupting the Brandfort blacks and giving them ideas above their station. They demanded that she be removed from their midst. But presumably the South African government could think of nowhere more isolated and desolate than Brandfort because they kept Winnie there in spite of the fierce objections of the white townsfolk.

A former state president of South Africa, the late Mr "Blackie" Swart (the word swart means black in Afrikaans), had a large farm in the Brandfort district. When he drove into town he insisted on being accompanied by an armed guard in case he was confronted by the "dangerous terrorist" in their midst—a precaution that made even the Afrikaners of Brandfort smile. (South Africa has not had much luck with its state presidents in the 23 years since a republic was declared. Mr Swart's successor, Dr N. Diederichs, a former Minister of Finance, died a bankrupt owing large sums and with rumours flying around of millions lodged in Switzerland. Later came Mr B. J. Vorster, former Prime Minister, who resigned in disgrace, after the shortest of tenures, when the Department of Information scandal broke and he was implicated, with rumours of further millions stashed in Paraguay. The post has now been abolished and replaced by that of executive president.)

Blacks in Brandfort who had expected, from the official description, that Mrs Mandela would be some fearful creature to be shunned at all costs, were amazed at the reality and riveted by the impact she made in the town. For the first time in their lives they saw a black person unafraid to deal with whites on an equal level and to argue with them till she got her way. They would trail after her around the streets, intrigued by her striking appearance and that of her attractive young daughter. They gasped when she insisted on trying on a dress in a shop before making a purchase—something forbidden till then. When children walked past her house, staring in wide-eyed curiosity, Winnie listened to their conversation as they talked among themselves. Within days she was picking up Tswana and when mothers approached tentatively, ostensibly to collect their children, Winnie tried talking to them. More and more women stopped to exchange a few words as they walked past her house, soon realizing that this new arrival was not the fearsome person the authorities had depicted.

Then one day, when a child cut her foot on a broken bottle in the street nearby, Winnie carried her into her house to clean, anoint and bandage the wound. That simple act of first aid wiped out any remaining doubts about Winnie. She herself believes that incident marked the start of her acceptance.

When reports of the grim conditions at Winnie's place of banishment evoked sympathy from many parts, reporters and photographers swarmed into Brandfort for more news of her, leaving the white residents of the sleepy little town bemused and the blacks amazed and intrigued. Almost overnight Winnie had put the drab little town on the map—which was not at all what had been intended.

With donations from well-wishers she was able to buy items of furniture that would fit into her dwelling, gradually making it more habitable. "But to me it will always be a prison," says Winnie. "I am watched all the time. To begin with they had a security policeman standing outside my house all day long as well as a police van patrolling the road every fifteen minutes. After my lawyer complained they moved the watcher to a hill opposite and now they scan this place through binoculars all the time."

Though she was living in such an isolated area and was confined to the house every night and throughout weekends the constant vigil was never relaxed. Zinzi complained that the police visited the house several times a day. "They never leave my mother alone," she said at the time.

When Winnie opened the cupboard in which her provisions were stored at the police station she found that rats had invaded everything. Her month's supply of perishable groceries, which she had bought before she was removed from Johannesburg, and which the police had packed up with her other possessions, was ruined. The rats had tunnelled their way into the flour, sugar, porridge, pulses and anything edible, even gnawing through wood to get at the food, damaging furniture and irreplaceable items. "Those rodents ate their way through Nelson's law books as though instructed by the Minister of Justice himself," says Winnie.

Soon afterwards Winnie learnt from friends in Johannesburg why her furniture had been removed so swiftly and in its entirety from her Orlando West home. A security policeman and his family had been installed in the house. Winnie was furious. The house had been leased to Nelson for his lifetime by the Johannesburg Municipality many years previously and no one else had the right to occupy it without permission. She instructed her lawyer to evict the new occupants. It was a year later before this was achieved but once the house was empty again the police loaded all Winnie's furniture they held in storage into a van and carted it back to Johannesburg and the Orlando West house.

When police in Brandfort saw how township residents were beginning to congregate around Winnie's house, even wandering inside to talk to her, they decided something must be done to keep people out. A sturdy wire fence was erected in front of her plot. Winnie was delighted and even more so, when, after foreign newspaper reports had criticized the dilapidated condition of neighbouring houses, similar fences were erected at all the homes in the vicinity of Winnie's. People living further afield and out of view were not so lucky. They were left unfenced and neglected. The fences were, says Winnie, the first improvements made in the township in 50 years. Her stock was rising. No longer was she a pariah but someone who got things done.

Eyes goggled when workmen arrived to lay water pipes from the street to Winnie's house. Yet, far from being intended as a concession, this was done as another move to isolate the exile. The police had been waging a constant battle with Winnie over her insistence on collecting water at the street tap after 6 p.m.—the start of the period when she was forbidden to leave her house or consort with anyone. Winnie was not to be gainsaid. If she needed water, which she did every night, she would stride out defiantly with her bucket to collect it—order or no order. Threats were to no avail. It was noticed, too, that whenever Winnie queued for water now there was always laughter and animated conversation around her. It sent her jailers into a huddle debating how best to force her to remain indoors in the evenings. Their solution was a triumph for Winnie when they decided she must be provided with her own water supply within the confines of her own plot. That would prevent her mixing with and corrupting other householders. The water was connected to a tap outside her kitchen—the only house in the township to have a tap of its own. It was a wonderful boost to Winnie's morale—which had certainly not been the intention.

Chapter Thirteen

WHILE ZINZI WAS sharing her mother's ordeal in Brandfort, Winnie's elder daughter, Zeni, was leading a very different life. Now eighteen, she had completed her schooling at Waterford and was engaged to Prince Thumbumuzi Dhlamini, 58th son of King Sobhuza II of Swaziland. King Sobhuza had scores of wives and hundreds of children but only the names of the sons were recorded in order of their appearance in the world—and upon their marriage each was accorded the pomp and ceremony of a royal marriage.

Winnie's attempts to get permission to visit Swaziland for the wedding failed and she had almost resigned herself to missing her daughter's marriage when she heard that King Sobhuza himself had approached the South African government for permission for her to visit his realm. The government obviously considered it diplomatic to accede to this request from a neighbouring country and to Winnie's delight she was notified that she could go.

Almost simultaneously Kaiser Matanzima, at that time Prime Minister of the Transkei which had been granted "independence" the previous year, asked permission for Winnie to visit the Transkei to sort out family business connected with the marriage. Elated at this unexpected respite from her grim surroundings Winnie set off only to find—much to her chagrin—that her presence in the Transkei was merely a formality. Instead of being involved in organizing the wedding she was simply told about the arrangements which were in the hands of Kaiser and Paramount Chief Sabata Dalindyebo. In Nelson's absence they had absolute rights over the Thembu children, according to custom, while their mother had no say at all. It was a bitter pill for an emancipated woman to swallow but Winnie knew there was nothing she could do about it.

Kaiser chartered a plane to fly him to Swaziland to negotiate the terms of Zeni's marriage on behalf of her imprisoned father. And he assigned a retinue of Thembu chiefs to accompany Winnie and her daughters to Swaziland for the celebrations. It is indicative of the close family

151

connections among the Xhosas that, even though Nelson and Kaiser are diametrically opposed in their political views, when it comes to matters affecting Nelson's family Kaiser takes upon himself the responsibility for attending to them without allowing political feelings to intrude.

Winnie had always been refused a passport so she had no travel papers for crossing into another country, yet when she and her escort arrived at the border the gates were simply opened to allow her through without any formalities. Twenty large government limousines were awaiting her arrival, and as soon as she crossed the border the drivers sounded their horns in unison to welcome her. "It must have been heard throughout the whole kingdom," laughs Winnie.

She was overwhelmed by the pomp accorded her as the bride's mother. Zeni was whisked away by a waiting group of her future sisters-in-law to be prepared in customary manner for the ceremony—leaving Winnie and Zinzi to receive red-carpet treatment. Winnie was told that this was the first time that one of the Swazi princes had chosen a blue-blooded bride (Nelson being of the Thembu royal house). In addition, she says, King Sobhuza was one of the oldest and staunchest members of the African National Congress so the marriage had political connotations, too.

In the future the ageing king was to bow to pressure from South Africa and refuse to allow ANC officials to operate or even to live in Swaziland, but at the time of the wedding all was amity and accord. A special state reception was given by the monarch in Winnie's honour. "I have never encountered such splendour and glamour," recalls Winnie. "I was treated to everything that was most modern in a nation that was supposed to be culturally retrogressive. But I had been out of the social scene for so long that I was quite bemused by all the pomp. At the banquet Zinzi had to kick me under the table to draw my attention to the waiter hovering patiently behind me waiting to pour my wine. And I had not realized that the whole assembly was waiting for me, as the guest of honour, to give the go ahead for everyone to start eating the lavish food provided."

Zeni's wedding, in traditional Swazi style, was vastly different from her mother's. It started in the royal kraal before sunrise. Zeni was woken at 4 a.m. by a large group of young women and taken down to the river to be bathed before dawn broke. Then, dressed only in a skirt, she was put through all the ritual ceremonies for a Swazi royal bride. The bridegroom's role was simply to sit and look on! Winnie was delighted with her new son-in-law, who is in banking, and happy to leave Zeni in his care.

Heartened by the reception she had received in Swaziland she returned to Brandfort refreshed, only to be struck anew by the desolation and air of hopelessness in the township. The fact that she had been dumped in Brandfort to demoralize her made her determined to prove that it was possible to rise above even those grim surroundings and primitive living conditions. However, the challenge was to prove more daunting than she had at first anticipated. Her initial anger and indignation soon gave way to a sense of gloom at the prospect of living out her days in such surroundings.

Having spent so much of her life in the invigorating environment of a large city she was particularly affected by the isolation that now enveloped her. Friends, perhaps inevitably, with their jobs to consider and their own lives to lead, made the arduous trek into the Free State to visit her increasingly less frequently. The local newsagent stocked only right-wing Afrikaans-language newspapers and even those arrived one and sometimes two days later. Fortunately she had her radio to keep abreast of news in the world outside.

Though she had succeeded in befriending a number of people in the township—for she could now speak their language passably well—the differences in their backgrounds became increasingly apparent. She craved for the intellectual stimulation she had always enjoyed in Soweto and for the political ferment and activity of her past. Knowing it would be easy to degenerate into aimlessness and apathy she was determined to avoid such a slide. To begin with she set about making basic household improvements.

Shortly after her return from Swaziland a friend of Zinzi, Johannes Seakamela, arrived on a visit. He was clever with his hands so Winnie seized the opportunity to get him to do odd jobs about the house. Her first priority was an indoor water supply to save having to step outside for every drop they needed. Johannes bored a hole in the kitchen wall and connected up the outside tap to the kitchen and installed an outlet pipe so that Winnie could fit a sink and have running water inside. That little amenity made an enormous difference. Johannes helped to put up shelves, to carpet the floor and, together, they stencilled a pattern on the lounge walls to resemble wallpaper.

Gradually, as money became available, Winnie added necessities such as a paraffin refrigerator, another stove and little comforts that made life much easier. A marmalade cat installed himself and a gift of some hens was housed in a coop at the back. Johannes cemented a path from the door to the gate and Zinzi wrote their names in the wet cement outside the kitchen.

As her home slowly became more habitable Winnie took stock of the situation, realizing the full extent of the adjustment required of her if she were to continue to serve her people. It required a plan of action quite different to any she had followed in Johannesburg—she would have to motivate and educate the townsfolk in a way that would have some direct bearing on their daily lives of misery.

"The greatest problem was overcoming their state of abject submission, born of years and years in this backwater," she says. "It would have been quite useless simply to have lectured them on the evils of apartheid and the need to throw off the yoke of oppression. Their own circumstances taught me far more about oppression and exploitation than I could ever have told them. I felt that somehow I had to rekindle their confidence in their own ability and worth; I had to involve them in projects that would help alleviate their dreadful conditions and, at the same time, unite them as a community."

As an experienced social worker she could see countless avenues for putting her training to good use by involving the shack dwellers in a self-help programme to lift them out of their despair. Now that she had a tap in her ground she began to set an example by turning her plot into a garden and then encouraging others to follow suit. Often visitors from the cities who called to see Winnie took her gifts of fruit and, with the frugality learnt in childhood, she saved and planted the stones. It was just a little activity to help pass the lonely hours but it proved a fruitful one in every sense. The stones sprang up into sturdy saplings. She planted a selection in the ground alongside her house and, because she still had dozens of tiny fruit trees to be transplanted, she distributed them among people who lived nearby. Her neighbours on both sides were security policemen, strategically placed to keep an eye on her, but their initial hostility dissipated gradually as their wives and children began visiting socially. Tensions eased and when Winnie offered to plant some of her trees in their gardens the men were glad to accept the offer. Soon there were fruit trees taking root alongside several of the houses and within a few years Winnie had the satisfaction and pleasure of helping to pick a wonderful crop of peaches.

At first, however, her little trees looked naked and forlorn in their barren surroundings, so she decided there must be a lawn to set them off. Inspiration for this came from the sight of patches of grass that sprang up beneath the constantly dripping communal taps at the sides of the township streets. With the aid of a spade and a wheelbarrow Winnie set to work on the start of what became known as her garden project. Painstakingly she dug out turves of grass beneath the nearest tap, placing them carefully in the barrow and wheeling them home to plant in her plot. They made a pitifully small patch but, nothing daunted, she trundled the barrow down the road and round the corner to the next tap and so on until she had lifted up the grass from beneath each one. It was backbreaking work but worth the trouble, for the final result was an impressive instant lawn, transforming her plot and the verge beyond her fence. The greensward was like an oasis in the desert. No longer did she need to describe to visitors the way to her house. They had only to drive until they reached the house with a garden.

Now that she had proved her desert could be made to bloom Winnie asked a group of township women to join her in starting to grow vegetables. The Council of Churches, hearing of her efforts, sent a generous gift of seeds to distribute among the women. Many were too apathetic to bother to plant these but others responded and, where once there had been just barren wasteland, patches of green appeared. A start had been made and Winnie knew the results would encourage others even though the prolonged drought was to prove a severe setback.

Her lawn was such a novelty to the children of the neighbourhood that it drew them like a magnet. Soon there was always a cluster of them playing on the grass. Winnie took to advising mothers on their nutrition and before long women were taking their babies with increasing frequency to her door for instruction on feeding or for treatment when they were sick.

"Some of the white doctors in the town set aside periods after 5 p.m., when the white patients have gone home, for 'kaffir' visits for cash only, but few blacks can afford to consult a doctor and when I saw how they queued up to ask my advice about their ailments it gave me the idea of starting a home clinic," says Winnie. She told visitors who travelled to see her of this idea and Dr Motlana, Archdeacon Rushton and others provided her with basic medical supplies so that she could minister to the sick. Often she used donations from well-wishers to buy baby food to reduce the high infant mortality, as fresh milk in Brandfort was too expensive for them to buy.

As word spread, the sick and injured made a beeline for Winnie's door. Frequently the security police would take the names of those waiting to see her (the patients had to be seen singly as she was forbidden to be in the company of more than one person at a time) but police interest failed to scare off those seeking her help. Later, when a large donation of money arrived from abroad, Winnie decided to spend it on a second-hand kombi to use as a mobile clinic. It was also used to deliver medical supplies to labourers on outlying farms and in Brandfort itself, and to transport more serious cases to a doctor in Bloemfontein.

Winnie treats simple ailments such as coughs, colds and stomach disorders and gives first aid to the injured. For want of anywhere else to keep the medical supplies donated by friends, she had to keep these for years on top of a cupboard in her tiny lounge. The supplies are delivered by her lodger, Matthews Kganitsiwe, a young artist friend of Winnie's two daughters, who arrived on a visit and stayed on to become major domo in the household.

MK, as he is called, has been struggling for years to obtain papers to regularize his life and enable him to live somewhere legally—without avail. He was arrested at Winnie's home and charged with being there illegally but the court ruled that as a member of the household he was entitled to stay there as a lodger. He has been there ever since, taking care of many chores and filling in his time by painting, the sale of his pictures bringing him in a small income.

Many of the elderly people who queued at Winnie's door for medical treatment were simply starving. They would beg for something to eat. To help them she decided to open a soup kitchen. Now when sympathizers asked what she needed she invariably said soup powder. Her first gift of this kind came from the Black Sash and when the large sacks arrived she set up her soup kitchen with a group of the more motivated township women who had offered to help, operating from the mobile clinic's kombi. Initially it was intended to feed only pre-school children, the aged and the completely destitute. "But," said Winnie, explaining her predicament to a soup donor, "when the children walk miles to come to school here because they have heard there is soup, what can you do? You cannot turn them away hungry. Today we served a hundred this morning and another eighty this afternoon. Sometimes we run out of soup powder altogether and have to wait for some kind person to donate more. With the drought on, the wealthy farmers around here are killing off their cattle and they and the butchers could well afford to give bones for us to make soup ourselves but they do not regard us as human beings—only as a work force."

Winnie was shocked to discover that several of the malnourished children in the township had been fathered by white Boers (as she calls the Afrikaners) in Brandfort. She says she is able to name the men involved—men who are not concerned that their illegitimate little half-caste children are starving. "They do not so much as acknowledge their existence."

While shopping in Brandfort one day Winnie was dismayed to see people buying bread by the slice because they could not even afford to buy half a loaf. It gave her the idea for her next project. She gathered together a group of women and put her plan to them—she would teach them to bake bread and they could open a bakery and sell their products to their fellow townsfolk at cost. The little bakery was an instant and continuing success.

Then came the idea for a sewing group which she holds in the nearby Methodist church hall. She is not allowed to demonstrate to a group so she sits in a back room while the women approach her from the hall, one by one, for instruction. "I teach them to sew, knit, crochet and embroider. Some of them are very good and we hope eventually to sell what they make but there is nowhere around here we can sell things," she says. The women showed their appreciation of her efforts by making her gifts of bead jewellery in the yellow, green and black colours of the outlawed ANC.

Well-wishers who heard of the sewing group came up trumps once again. Professor Harvey van der Merwe, a Quaker attached to the University of Cape Town, provided two new sewing machines and, with donations, Winnie bought four more second-hand ones that are used by about 20 women. Her attorney in Johannesburg, Ismail Ayob, sent a big blot of black cloth to make tunics for the schoolchildren and the sewing group was off to an encouraging start.

Winnie was working in her garden one day when she heard piercing screams coming from the wasteland opposite. She rushed across in time to save an eleven-year-old from being raped. On discovering that the child was an orphan Winnie took her into her home to care for her. That girl was the first of a string of waifs and young offenders to whom Winnie has given shelter and tried to rehabilitate since she arrived in Brandfort. The offenders sometimes slip back into their old ways but Winnie is not discouraged.

Her first case, the little girl she saved from rape, spent several years with Winnie who sent her to school and was delighted with her progress till at fourteen she fell pregnant. Winnie continued to give her a home and after the baby was born and weaned she sent the mother back to school. "But what is she to do afterwards?" asks Winnie. "There is no work for her. All I can do is teach her hygiene and to knit, sew, and cook so that she has some skills."

Winnie's friends shake their heads in amused disbelief at her perseverance with her delinquents, as they are called. Yet to a born social worker they are a challenge on her doorstep that she is not prepared to ignore. "Her optimism is quite irrepressible," says Dr Motlana. "It is we who go to visit her who are depressed at her surroundings. She is always so bright—nothing seems to get her down. She makes us feel quite humble." Winnie herself modestly attributes her determination and optimism to the example she says she finds in Nelson.

Political prisoners released from Robben Island over the years made a point of contacting Winnie with first-hand accounts of Nelson's activities there. She learnt that even though he and the other Rivonia "lifers" were kept isolated from the main body of prisoners, all those serving sentences on the island regarded Nelson as their leader and he never failed them. He directed their activities, encouraged them to occupy their spare time in study and other worthwhile pursuits and to participate in sport. If there were disputes it was to Nelson they turned to settle them. Those who have been allowed to visit Nelson have been astonished at the way he refused to allow himself to deteriorate in prison and at the continuing grasp he has of South African and world affairs. Through the bush telegraph he is kept in touch, not only with events but with public reaction to them.

Four years ago Dr Motlana was able to see Nelson on Robben Island in connection with the guardianship of his children and he was staggered to see his old friend so little changed. "It was absolutely amazing to find Nelson, after sixteen years, looking almost the same. He was upright and confident to the point of arrogance—what tremendous self-confidence! He deliberately assumed a Xhosa accent when speaking to me. It was wonderful to see him again but the visit was a frustrating one as we were only allowed to discuss the children and nothing else. When that subject was exhausted I started to chat about boxing as Nelson used to do amateur boxing in Orlando—I remember what a frightening sight he was in the ring with his huge six-foot three-inch frame—but they wouldn't even allow me to talk about such an innocent subject."

Dr Motlana, as chairman of Soweto's Committee of Ten, has his finger on the pulse of popular feeling there. Youngsters growing up who have never seen Nelson or Winnie, nor heard them speak, still regarded them as their leaders, he says.

Though Nelson has been imprisoned for nearly a quarter of a century, with South African newspapers forbidden by law to publish anything he says or writes, frequent opinion polls show that he remains the most popular leader in South Africa. Kaiser Matanzima in the Transkei and Gatsha Buthelezi in Zululand, who are able to issue their own brand of propaganda to encourage followers, both lag far behind Nelson in the popularity stakes. Even though they claim to espouse the cause of democracy and liberation their action in collaborating with the government by working within the apartheid system has disgusted the majority who are solidly behind Nelson and the banned ANC.

Nelson has earned widespread respect, even from political opponents, for his persistent refusal to accept "freedom" on terms that would cause him to compromise his views. South African government ministers and Kaiser Matanzima have pleaded with Nelson to agree to eschew all political activity and retire to the Transkei, but this he will not do. Winnie, too, is contemptuous of overtures that have been made to her to end her banishment by voluntarily agreeing to live in Swaziland and, when this failed, in the Transkei. "Matanzima and I have had violent exchanges from time to time," she says. "He makes out that I and his uncle [Nelson] are terrorists. We see each other from time to time because we are family—you can't disguise that fact—but politically we are poles apart."

Of the South African government's suggestion that she should go to live in Swaziland, Winnie, her sense of humour deserting her for once, rages: "How dare a racist, fascist, minority settler regime offer me passage out of the very country it stole from me. The arrogance of that is beyond my comprehension. If anyone should leave my country it is the settlers. The masses are offering them the choice of doing that if they do not want to accept our generosity to share the wealth of our land and the power that rightly belongs to us."

Chapter Fourteen

THE 1980s USHERED in a new era in the course of events in Southern Africa. In Rhodesia, after nearly fourteen years of UDI and a protracted and bloody civil war, the minority government of Ian Smith came to an end—an event of particular significance to South Africans. When the Zanu PF party of Robert Mugabe won a landslide victory in the Zimbabwe elections this was greeted in South Africa with delight by the blacks and with alarm and dismay by many whites. The South African government was said to have invested millions of rands in Bishop Abel Muzorewa's election campaign in the hope of ensuring a compliant administration in the newly independent state. His overwhelming defeat added impetus to the growing mood of resistance in South Africa.

In April 1980 there began a period of unrest among blacks and coloureds throughout the country that was to bring vicious clampdowns by the police in an effort to contain the trouble which today appears to have become endemic.

It started with a schools boycott against apartheid education and resulted in the widespread closure of black and coloured schools, training colleges and universities. In the midst of this upheaval thousands of blacks employed in major industries in Johannesburg went on strike. Whole areas were sealed off by the police, hundreds were detained throughout the country, and many were killed and injured when police fired on protesters. The situation became even more serious when thousands of black miners—the lifeblood of the country—joined the industrial unrest and were granted hasty concessions to prevent a major threat to the economy.

For Winnie, isolated in Brandfort, it was intensely frustrating to be distanced from these events and to be able to follow the progress of the unrest only through the government-controlled radio or the pro-government Afrikaans newspapers sold in Brandfort. She longed to be among the people. "Words cannot describe how helpless I feel at such times, stuck out here without regular contact with my people outside," she says.

On the personal side the opening of the decade was a sad time for Winnie. Her favourite sister, Nancy, died from leukaemia at the early age of forty-seven. Although Nancy had spent many years in exile across the border in neighbouring Botswana, only being allowed to return for a brief period when she was dying, she and Winnie had remained close, sharing their joys and sorrows, and her death was one of the severest blows Winnie had to suffer.

Finding the enforced idleness of her life increasingly frustrating Winnie's hopes of a job were raised when she heard that the Bloem-fontein Child Welfare Society was looking for a social worker. She applied and was offered the post but she was unable to take it up for when she sought permission to commute the 35 miles between Brandfort and Bloemfontein each day it was refused.

At this time she had long since successfully completed all the written requirements for her degree in social science through Unisa (University of South Africa). All that remained was for her to carry out a course of field work. But, because of her banning order, she is prohibited from meeting others in a group as required and the university authorities told her Brandfort was not a suitable area for case work, though Winnie considers it ideal. Undeterred by the inability to finalize her degree she simply switched courses to study politics and communications.

Fortunately her sense of humour has helped her enormously through the difficult years and she can usually find something to laugh at in the antics of the security police who dog her footsteps. One incident she always recalls with amusement concerns a white security policeman, Warrant Officer Gert Prinsloo. He was appointed to keep a constant watch on Winnie in Brandfort—even escorting her to the shops. But, says Winnie, this constant surveillance and the boredom of finding nothing untoward to report started to get Prinsloo down. He began drinking. One day he staggered into the house to say he had come to arrest MK.

"At the time MK was working quite openly in the garden but Prinsloo searched the house. He opened the doors of a tiny cupboard in the lounge (hardly big enough to hold a dog) and peered inside and then he got down on his knees, lifted the carpet and looked under that. When I asked him what he was doing he said he was looking to see if MK were hiding under there!

"I complained about his drunken behaviour and later his superior officer came to tell me that Prinsloo had been transferred—but he emphasized he had not been demoted, only transferred. His surveillance of me was more of a punishment for him than for me as he had to stand for hours in the blazing sun just watching my house. Even when I am sleeping I know there are security men outside. It is quite ridiculous."

In May 1981 Winnie obtained compensation for a series of libellous statements made in evidence to the Cillie Commission appointed to investigate the causes of the Soweto riots five years before. Newspapers had carried reports of the evidence of Dr Aaron Mthlare, Winnie's erstwhile friend and colleague, falsely incriminating and libelling her and his co-committee member, Dr Nthato Motlana. Dr Mthlare had claimed in his evidence that Winnie had planned the Soweto uprising and that he had heard her and Dr Motlana telling the students to attack government property, institutions and bottle stores. For good measure he had added that Winnie and Dr Motlana were having an affair.

It was too much for Winnie. She was incensed at the string of lies, particularly as Dr Mthlare had been closely connected with her in the Black Parents Association as well as in the ANC; he had been working alongside her in the aftermath of the riots and he had been detained with her and other members of the BPA a month later. She instructed her lawyer to sue for defamation and she and Dr Motlana took the case to the Supreme Court where Dr Mthlare was ordered to pay each of them R3,000 damages and publicly to apologize and withdraw unreservedly all the allegations he had made.

Winnie was puzzled, as she knew Dr Mthlare was well aware of both her true role in the events of 1976 and the long-standing friendship she and Nelson had with Dr Motlana and his wife, Sally. For Dr Mthlare to allege there had been impropriety between her and Dr Motlana was so absurd that she knew there must be something more behind this. She instigated some inquiries which revealed that, when Dr Mthlare had been detained after the Soweto uprising, he had broken down under torture and agreed to give false evidence against his friends. Winnie believes the substantial sum of money he was ordered to pay in compensation was provided by the police.

Dr Mthlare and his wife subsequently left South Africa to live in Botswana, away from the recriminations of one-time friends, though Winnie is now understanding of the pressures that forced him to such perfidy. Though she seldom forgets a wrong she has an amazing capacity for forgiveness in the case of her countrymen who fall into the hands of the security police and find themselves being "turned" against their will. "I know the tactics of the security police," she will say. "Their victims cannot help it. Not everyone has the strength to hold out. I don't think people overseas realize just how many people have actually died in detention. It is one thing to shoot a person but another thing entirely to torture them until they die. That is not human."

She pauses as if to shut out the thought. In Winnie's case it must be a particularly frightening one: the possibility of her own assassination is never remote. In recent years several close friends were murdered by, she believes, South African agents. In 1981 Joe Gqabi, the ANC chief representative in Zimbabwe, was shot dead in the street and later that year Griffiths Mxenge, a prominent Durban attorney, was found severely mutilated near his office.

In May 1982 Winnie received an anonymous threatening letter reminding her of how two close acquaintances of hers, Petrus Nzima and his wife, had been killed by a car-bomb in Swaziland and warning that a similar fate awaited her and Zinzi.

"Not even innocent postcards sent to me through the post escape interception, yet the security police hadn't even opened this letter. I can only presume it was because they already knew its contents," she says. At the time she did not take the threats too seriously as her life has been threatened many times in order to scare her. However, a few days later when she tried to start the mobile clinic kombi, as was her practice every morning, she found that detonator leads had been connected to the battery. Neighbours told her that late the previous night they had disturbed several men crouching at the kombi and had interrupted them in their work. Neighbours believe the men were fixing the vehicle to blow up when started.

Friends immediately saw to it that the threats were published in newspapers overseas and nothing more came of them. But only two months later a former Treason Trialist and prominent anti-apartheid activist, Ruth First, was killed by a parcel bomb sent to her office in Maputo.

It is Winnie's extraordinary resilience in the face of unrelenting harassment and intimidation that has focused international attention on her as well as on Nelson. As a banned person she cannot be quoted in South Africa but no such restriction exists abroad where her treatment has aroused considerable indignation. Diplomats from virtually every accredited embassy in South Africa have contacted her in Brandfort. The German ambassador has been particularly generous in driving out to visit her and sending streams of food parcels for the township residents. He also gave her a television set and a large battery to run it off as there was no electricity. It has proved a never-ending source of wonder and delight to the township residents who crowd into her tiny lounge to watch it while Winnie, to conform to her banning order, stays in the other room. She is far from overawed by all the diplomatic attention. Forthright as ever, she told the American representatives not to call again, thus expressing her displeasure at President Reagan's policies.

In October 1982, five years and five months after the start of her banishment, Winnie's attorney in Brandfort, Piet de Waal, called at her house on a matter requiring her signature. He found her tossing deliriously in bed with a raging fever. The local white doctor was fetched immediately. He gave her emergency treatment but, he said, she needed to go into hospital at once as her life was in danger. Permission had to be sought both to move her from Brandfort to the nearest hospital and for her to be admitted to the exclusively white Universitas Boere Hospital in Bloemfontein. When she heard this Winnie refused point-blank to go to the all-white hospital. Nor would she consider the hospital for blacks in Bloemfontein where, she said, the patients were treated like cattle.

With that stubborn streak her father had recognized so many years ago she insisted on being treated by her own doctor in a hospital of her choice in Johannesburg or not at all. In vain did the doctor and her lawyer urge her to agree to go to Bloemfontein. They pointed out she could die through her intractability. Winnie was adamant: Johannesburg or nothing. This put the authorities in a real quandary. By now the name of Winnie Mandela was so well known internationally that they could not risk letting her die and have the world say she was refused permission to have the treatment she wanted. The doctor in Brandfort reported that her infection was brought on by the primitive conditions under which she had been living for so long. Eventually the authorities gave in and issued a permit for Winnie to leave Brandfort temporarily. She was flown to Johannesburg where she was admitted to the Rosebank Clinic, a privately owned institution that did not require special permission to admit non-whites.

Winnie's leg was acutely infected and after it had been operated on she spent seven weeks in hospital. Throughout that time, even though she was incapable of moving, the security police kept up a constant vigil, monitoring the arrival of any visitors calling to see her. Her Johannesburg attorney, Ismail, and his wife, Zamila, visited her every single day of the seven weeks she was in hospital. One day when Ismail arrived for his usual visit there was a "No visitors" sign on the door. On making inquiries he was told Winnie was too ill to see anyone. But he knew from his visit the previous day that she was recovering and insisted on going into her room. There he found her sitting up in bed progressing well. He tackled the matron about the "No visitors" notice, accusing her of pandering to the security police. Though she denied this the police subsequently took care to avoid being seen by Ismail.

The watchman at the Rosebank Clinic grumbled that the police were standing around all the time "interfering with his work"! They only moved, he said, when they saw the tall attorney approaching. Then they would scurry round the corner and hide until he had gone.

A nurse at the clinic who was seen talking to Winnie was threatened with dismissal for carrying on a conversation with the patient. Ismail, complained to the matron about that incident, too—asking her since when had she started taking her instructions from the security police. Again she denied it, but at the end of Winnie's stay she gave Ismail a ten per cent discount on the hospital fees. He took that to be by way of a tacit apology. On her discharge from the hospital no fewer than five police cars were waiting to follow Ismail as he drove her to the airport. "It was terribly flattering," laughs Winnie. "Sometimes I wonder if they were trained in Texas that they operate on such a scale."

By a stroke of fate the flight to Bloemfontein was fully booked so Ismail and his wife took Winnie back to their flat to spend the night. They soon realized that she was still in a deplorably weak state and in no condition to undertake the flight back to Bloemfontein to fend for herself in Brandfort. Permission was sought for her to recuperate at her old home in Orlando West until she was strong enough to return to her place of banishment but this was refused. The police insisted that if she did so she would be charged with breaking her banning order. (Later that did happen and she was convicted.)

Nevertheless, the next day Ismail drove Winnie to Soweto, followed again by several police cars, and once again she entered the home from which she had been taken so summarily in 1977. "But it was not the same," says Winnie. "The thought that it had been occupied by the police—that my oppressors had lived in it for almost a year—made me feel completely alienated from the house. I imagine I must have felt the way people in Europe felt during the German occupation when Nazis invaded their homes and turned them into billets for soldiers.

"I found that Soweto itself had changed, changed immeasurably: not the tiny, overcrowded houses or the pot-holed roads or the long train and bus queues, but the attitudes of the people there.

"They came to see me in their hundreds. They stormed into the house, braving the wrath of the security police, even though they could only enter my room singly which was the condition of my stay as far as my legal team was concerned.

"Harold Wilson once said that a week in politics is a long time. Well, I had been away for five and a half years. I had tried to keep in touch with individuals and events but it is not the same thing as being there in person and sensing the mood of the people. Coming to it afresh after so long I was staggered at the way feelings had hardened.

"I don't think the whites have any idea of how they are polarizing the people in the land. The Sowetans are bitter—far more bitter than prior to the 1976 uprising—and their resentment of all that has happened since 1976 is far too deep-rooted to be changed by any more government promises.

"They know that majority rule is their right and they are determined to have it at any cost. The government seems to think that by imprisoning our leaders, banning our organizations and smashing our strikes they can stem the tide of history. No one has ever been able to do that," she asserts.

"I found that the regime's ploy of creating a buffer pseudo-middle class of blacks through the Urban Foundation and like organizations is regarded by the very people who benefit from it as a monumental fraud. This fight for our country is a fight all the way and it is no longer a matter of any consequence to me where I fight from. The fascist government seems to think that by forcing the front-line states into denying the ANC any support they will halt the forces of change. But the people inside this country are as determined as ever to claim their rights. Through all these years I have never had any doubts that the day will come when Nelson will come out to lead our people with my brother, Oliver Tambo."

Chapter Fifteen

WHEN WINNIE EVENTUALLY returned to Brandfort after her long illness she found herself more restricted than ever because her bad leg made it impossible for her to walk all the way to the white town to use the post office telephone. Her own application for a telephone in her home was refused—she believes because the authorities had taken so much trouble installing a recording system at the post office call boxes which they were not prepared to duplicate in the black township for her convenience.

When Nelson heard of his wife's difficulty in getting about he asked his attorney to use the money from a substantial award made to him by the Austrian government to buy a motor car for Winnie. The award money did not fully cover the cost of the new car so the balance was made up by Dr Motlana, Yusuff Cachalia, a former National Executive member of the ANC with Nelson, and by his attorney, Ismail. Soon a gleaming red Audi was delivered to No. 802 amid gasps of admiration from the black townspeople to whom this was further proof of Winnie's influence.

It says much for her popularity and influence that there is no jealousy when she receives gifts—probably because she is always so generous in sharing everything with those less fortunate than herself. As soon as money comes in it is spent on something for the good of the community. Gifts of clothing and food are distributed unstintingly to the most needy.

Soon after Winnie's return to Brandfort the security police arrived at her house to issue her with a summons (as they had threatened in Johannesburg) for breaking her banning order by staying in her Orlando home to recuperate. At the same time they raided her little home once again. On her bed was her bedspread crocheted in the yellow, green and black colours of the banned ANC. Indignantly they whipped this off the bed for confiscation and when their search uncovered the pieces of bead jewellery in ANC colours made for her by the grateful townsfolk, these too were confiscated.

That petty action was to have unexpected repercussions. News reports

167

ridiculing the police action prompted American sympathizers to announce they would replace the confiscated cover with another symbolic bedspread. They chose one in an old Pennsylvania design said to keep evil spirits at bay. Twenty-six leading senators and congressmen signed the bedspread which reached South Africa with all the attendant publicity Americans love. Mrs Helen Suzman, MP, who has spoken up for the Mandelas in parliament on many occasions, was detailed to hand the bedspread to Winnie in Brandfort.

Winnie's attitude towards Mrs Suzman is one of accord and gratitude for her efforts to help but when it comes to her feelings about the Progressive Federal Party, of which Mrs Suzman is probably the best-known representative, she is unequivocal in her condemnation.

"The PFP is such a waste," she says. "Though one cannot dismiss the part they have played in highlighting the plight of blacks in this country, they are of no relevance to our cause. No matter how much sympathetic and democratic posturing a political party engages in, once it is totally opposed to one man one vote and to the complete sharing of power and wealth in this country, as is the PFP, it automatically joins the ranks of the oppressors.

"Look how we have been calling for an end to foreign investment in this country on the grounds that it serves to strengthen the apartheid economy and so makes our struggle for democracy all the more difficult. The PFP is the party of Anglo-American big business, so they ignore our demands and travel the world telling people what fantastic profits can be made by investing in South Africa. Of course they say they are opposed to apartheid, but they shy away from the point that these super-profits are only possible because apartheid generates a virtually limitless supply of cheap black labour.

"They spend far more time and energy agonizing over the issue of white minority rights in any future constitution than they spend bringing about the conditions for an acceptable constitution. The surest guarantee of rights is a system based on equality and democracy in which everyone, regardless of colour or creed, is free to participate according to his or her ability."

The politics of exclusivity preached by the Azanian People's Organization (Azapo), which goes to the other extreme, are also condemned by Winnie.

"This is not the first time blacks have become frustrated and disillusioned with the slow progress and have resorted to extremist views," she says. "Azapo is continuing where Robert Sobukwe left off—and he died a mute martyr." (Sobukwe, leader of the PAC, advocated non-co-operation with whites and broke away from the ANC on that issue.) "When the situation is taking so long to resolve it is a natural and logical reaction for some people to feel so extremist and to scream inverted racist slogans.

"Nelson once made a speech titled 'No Easy Walk to Freedom', in which he pointed out that the struggle for our liberation would be a long and arduous one and that the people must guard against being diverted from the ultimate goal by the obstacles and lures in the path. It is a pity those in Azapo have not paid more heed to his advice for their policies can only lead to far, far more bitterness and bloodshed than is necessary."

In spite of constant government attempts to label both Winnie and Nelson as terrorists and communists, few outside white South African circles are deceived by this. Blacks in South Africa and the international community at large have come to recognize the couple by their actions and their statements as mature and responsible leaders.

Winnie herself is deeply religious. The only exception she has made to her determination not to ask for permission to go to church was when her grandchildren were being christened in Bloemfontein Cathedral by Archdeacon Rushton and the Revd Aidan Cross, Dean of Bloemfontein. Winnie felt she must attend so she sought permission to do so. But the security police were there too, and Winnie angrily describes their crudeness in leaning arrogantly against a wall in the cathedral during the service—never taking their eyes off her in case she spoke to someone during communion.

They were particularly watchful that she did not talk to Helen Joseph, a listed person. Helen is allowed to write to her friend but Winnie, as a banned person, may not reply, even to acknowledge a gift. Helen, now eighty and uncompromisingly committed to the anti-apartheid cause, is godmother to two of Winnie's grandchildren.

Over the years Winnie's household expanded in a way she had not envisaged. Zeni bore three children in quick succession and, according to custom, they were brought up in their early years by their maternal grandmother. Winnie adores children and having her own grandchildren to stay (Zinzi's two joined the others) has proved a tremendous solace—helping to make up for so much that she missed by being parted from her own daughters so often. The children stayed with Winnie till they were old enough to attend kindergarten. Now only the youngest is still with her and the others return in the school holidays. They call Winnie "Mama" and lead a happy and carefree existence under the watchful eye of MK or one of Winnie's "delinquents".

Over the years Winnie's visits to Nelson gradually became more frequent. At first she was allowed only one visit and one letter every six months, but as time passed he graduated to a better grade and was allowed the privilege of more frequent visits. His children, including his surviving son, Magatha, who works in Johannesburg, were also allowed to see him. The visits he did not welcome were the government-arranged ones by homeland leaders and successive South African Ministers of Justice whose sole purpose was to persuade him to give up all political involvement and live in obscurity—in which case he would be released. As his wife points out, he has given up a lifetime of freedom for his principles so he is unlikely to abandon them now. But she knows, too, how much it must cost him to refuse those offers, holding out as they do the chance of being with his family again.

Throughout his long imprisonment the police have tried hard to alienate Nelson from Winnie. Whenever anything derogatory to her appears in the newspapers the cutting is slipped under Nelson's cell door. But he is far too astute to be taken in by such ploys. It was he who warned Winnie to beware of scandalmongers and traps so he has been well able to cope with efforts to drive a wedge between them.

Any suggestion of Winnie's supposed infidelity would reach Nelson almost before it was uttered. This began with the case of the informer, Brian Somana, and was followed by many other allegations involving a wide range of men—some of whom she had never even heard of. Winnie soon learnt to ignore such lies, though many of the allegations made her rage. Taxed about these rumours of lovers in her life Winnie retorts that Nelson so completely fills her horizon that it is impossible to think of anyone else in that context.

Such is Nelson's charisma that even the once-hostile warders on Robben Island succumbed to him. One discharged prisoner described to Winnie how Nelson seemed to hold the warders in sway. He would sit on a stool and order his "boys", as he called the white warders, to do this or that and, to the amazement of the other prisoners, they would comply. In calling them boys Nelson was sending up the habit of white South Africans of calling grown black men "boy"—teaboy, kitchenboy, gardenboy, messengerboy or just boy. When the prison authorities realized the extent of Nelson's influence they took to changing the guards stationed on the island at frequent intervals.

Ismail, Nelson's Johannesburg attorney, was one day made graphically aware of the day-to-day deprivations endured by his client in a little incident that sticks in his mind. He had flown to Cape Town for a consultation with Nelson on Robben Island. Being pushed for time, he had taken with him some fruit and sandwiches for his lunch packed by his wife. He asked permission to share this with Nelson and the warders while they discussed the business in hand. When Ismail took out a banana from the picnic box he noticed the look of astonishment on Nelson's face. In a land where bananas grow wild as well as under cultivation in abundance, Nelson's comment was: "That is the first banana I have seen in twenty years."

As time went by Winnie never flagged in her efforts to bring about improvements to Nelson's life. Gradually the unrelieved drudgery endured by the political prisoners was eased and the grim conditions lightened. Much of this was due to the urgings of the Red Cross and the United Nations. Representatives of the International Red Cross began paying regular visits to the island and the prisoners were able to make known their complaints and requests to them.

Eventually the government gave in to pressure and allowed the men to study, to buy and use sports equipment and to have the occasional film show. After a mass hunger strike in the early days over the appalling food, that, too, was improved. Nelson did strenuous daily exercises to keep fit and studied diligently to exercise his mind while encouraging his fellow-prisoners to do the same.

It was only after he had been on the island for some time that Winnie learnt, with horror, of a second escape that had been planned for him which would have had a fatal ending. She read of the scheme in Gordon Winter's book. In it he described how people in England had planned an air rescue of Nelson from Robben Island. The South African government, claimed Winter, learnt of the plan while it was still in its early stages and decided it would be a good idea to let it go ahead right till the last minute when Nelson would be shot while boarding the escape plane. An ace British aviator, Miss Sheila Scott, was engaged as pilot but fortunately she backed out, the scheme had to be abandoned and Nelson's life was saved by default for the second time.

Over the years both Nelson and Winnie have received many international awards. Winnie was unable to accept hers in person as she was forbidden to leave the country. When Haverford Quaker College in Philadelphia notified her that she was to be awarded an honorary doctor of laws degree she asked her old friend, Adelaide Tambo, to accompany her elder daughter, Zeni, to receive the honour on her behalf. Zeni and her husband also visited Venezuela to receive the Simon Bolivar award for Nelson and in October 1984 they were the guests of the Danes to receive, on Winnie's behalf, the Freedom Prize awarded by Scandinavia's two chief liberal newspapers—the *Politiken* of Denmark and *Dagens Nyheter*, of Stockholm, Sweden. Winnie shared the prize with Helen Suzman who, like Zeni, visited Denmark for the occasion. Though Winnie could not be there the audience heard her voice in a tape-recorded message.

Zinzi has been unable to go overseas on her parents' behalf, even when the invitations have been addressed to her personally, because the South African government has persistently refused to give her travel documents. But Zeni's trips abroad have meant that she has been able to take messages to and from her mother and old friends in exile.

Some blacks in South Africa have condemned their colleagues living what they call lives of ease abroad, while those at home suffer for the cause. Winnie is not one of the critics. She is completely understanding of those who go into exile.

"In any revolutionary situation you need a government in exile. It is not necessary for everyone to be caught up in the crossfire. Everyone who has left the country has a role to play even if they don't appear to manifest that role in a way that can be seen.

"A decision to turn your back on your own country is traumatic and takes courage. To give up the comfort of being among familiar things and familiar people is not something you decide easily. From my own experience of being uprooted I know what it is like to leave everything behind. For me it is a scar that will never heal till vengeance is taken on those responsible. As far as that goes I will never turn the other cheek. I know there are those who will retaliate for me in generations to come even if I never have the satisfaction of doing so myself." This is one of those rare occasions when she suggests by implication that she may not still be around to see the fruition of her dreams.

Winnie's visits to Nelson would not have been possible without the donations from abroad to cover the high cost of her fares to and from the Cape. The Amalgamated Engineering Workers in Britain sent sufficient money to pay for eight visits. An anonymous donor in England sends regular contributions for her living expenses. She has tried hard to persuade the government to allow her to travel to Cape Town by train instead of by plane since the rail fare is only half the cost by air, but the government is adamant in its refusal. She must get from point to point in the shortest possible time.

Throughout the years when Winnie visited Nelson she had to travel straight from the airport to the police station in central Cape Town and then to the docks for the ferry ride. Afterwards she would go to a bleak coloured township called Elsie's River to spend the night with Dr Ayesha Ahmed and her doctor husband, friends whom the government apparently considers suitable chaperons for her. When she sought permission to spend the night with white friends this was refused.

So it came about that although she had been visiting Cape Town for 20 years to see her husband, it was only after he was transferred from the island to Pollsmoor Prison on the mainland that she had the chance to see the spectacularly beautiful southern suburbs of the land Sir Francis Drake dubbed "the Fairest Cape".

Pollsmoor Prison is a bleak edifice surrounded by a high brick wall close to the Tokai Forest and overlooked by towering Table Mountain. To reach it Winnie had to travel through the white suburbs of Rondebosch and Constantia along roadways banked with beautiful Cape flora—pincushion and sugarbush proteas, watsonias, heath and lovely old oaks planted by an earlier generation. For the first time she saw the weathered stone, creeper-covered buildings of the University of Cape Town which had honoured her years before by making her and her husband patrons of the debating society.

As she drove along the broad highway the lovely homes she passed only served to emphasize the contrast between this area and the dreary, unkempt-looking places on the outskirts where non-whites were forced to live. Sadly, Nelson did not even catch a glimpse of the beauties Winnie had admired on her drive to the prison. He was transported at dead of night in a closed van after landing from the ferry. With him were some of the other political prisoners serving life sentences—one of them his old friend, Walter Sisulu.

On her first visit to Nelson in Pollsmoor he used their precious time together to make a formal complaint for Winnie to pass on to his lawyer and the world outside about the deterioration in prison conditions that he and his colleagues were enduring. He told her it was obvious that the transfer had been for the purpose of inflicting further punishment. On

Robben Island they had had their own cells, were able to move around, mix with others and exercise in a wide area. In Pollsmoor six of them were now confined to one cell which they were not allowed to leave. Those who were not studying kept the prison-controlled radio blaring all the time—making it impossible for the two who were studying to concentrate. There was nowhere to exercise and they were no longer allowed to send or receive telegrams.

That last restraint was not as flippant as it sounds. Because letters often took as long as two months to go through the censors before being delivered it was customary in cases of urgent matters, such as a death in Nelson's or Winnie's family, to send notification by telegram. Winnie passed on the complaints to their lawyer and she also wrote to Nelson's biographer, Mary Benson, who lives in London. As a result articles about the deterioration in Mandela's prison conditions appeared in British newspapers. Whether it was overseas concern or his lawyer's representations—probably a combination of both—an improvement was made in Nelson's living conditions. Some of the stringent rules enforced were relaxed and it was a happier man Winnie saw on her next visit.

Despite his years of incarceration Nelson remains a devoted family man. The travails both he and Winnie have endured over the years have in no way overshadowed their concern and affection for their children.

Simply because she is their daughter, Zinzi has had to face her share of police harassment—something Zeni's marriage spared her. After writing her "O" levels at Waterford School in Swaziland in 1976 Zinzi spent some time with her mother in Brandfort. When she tried to return to her studies she found obstacles placed in her way at every turn. Chief among them was that she could not go in or out of Swaziland without a passport or travel papers and these the government refused to supply. Her efforts to obtain a pass (reference book) once she turned sixteen were thwarted at every turn, and without a pass she could not even obtain a driving licence, much less a passport.

Her repeated applications for a pass proved quite farcically frustrating. They dragged on for years, always with a new excuse being provided—first the application was lost; then the time for applying had expired before it could be processed; next she was advised to apply to the Transkei "homeland" for papers. This she refused to do because it would imply acceptance of her forfeiture of South African citizenship. Zinzi asked Mrs Suzman to help her get a pass but though Mrs Suzman tried, she was not successful. "They have it in for that whole family," she said.

In June 1981, when Zinzi was told she must start her application again from scratch—something that meant weeks more of queueing and waiting—she decided to take matters into her own hands. With something of her mother's ingenuity and persistence she obtained by unorthodox methods a legitimate travel document, and this she used to enter Swaziland to register at university there. On her return the ruse had been discovered, and she was arrested at the Oeshoek border post.

"I felt like a VIP with three men from the security police and two from the CID all having driven there to arrest little me," she recalls with a laugh. "They told me I was the indoctrinated one and asked me why I couldn't find myself a nice prince like my sister and stop troubling them."

Zinzi's travel document has puzzled the authorities and led to endless arguments. It is a legitimate document but Zinzi will not reveal how she came by it. While the police wanted her charged the prosecution considered there was no case to answer since the document was legitimate.

In the meantime she was released but with her travel document confiscated she was unable to return to Swaziland. She took a post at the Institute of Race Relations in Johannesburg, making the twelve-hour train ride to visit her mother in Brandfort at weekends. Now she is studying at the University of Cape Town.

Visits to her father have not been so frequent. She and Zeni had to wait till they were sixteen before being allowed to see him and then only through a glass partition. Until 1984 only Zeni had ever touched him since they were infants. Because of her marriage to Prince Thumbumuzi of Swaziland Zeni is entitled to diplomatic status when accompanied by her husband—hence she was allowed a contact visit to Nelson. Zinzi had to make her first visit to her father alone as her mother was not allowed to accompany her on that occasion.

"I had heard so much about my father that I was rather apprehensive about seeing him for the first time," she says. "He was more a great figure than a father. But when we met, even through the glass partition and speaking on telephones, I found it very easy. He is so versatile and charismatic that in just a few minutes he seemed to change the whole atmosphere. The warders were breathing down our necks all the time but he put me at my ease at once—recalling little incidents from the time when I was a baby.

"I have never touched him as Zeni has and I can only see him from the waist up, but I always feel close to him. He always asks me to stand and turn around so that he can see what I am wearing so I try to choose something special each time and to do my hair with beads which is what he likes.

"After my first visit alone I was allowed to accompany my mother but I found that a terribly embarrassing experience as my father and mother had eyes only for each other. They were so totally absorbed in each other that they were oblivious of anyone else. Because of that I decided my future visits would be alone so that I could claim my father's attention."

Their parents' constant imprisonment, banning and harassment have had an often traumatic effect on the two girls.

"I went to boarding school in Swaziland when I was only six," says Zinzi. "Since Mama was often in jail when the holidays came round we had to stay with a friend, Dr Alan Nxumalo, in Swaziland. He looked after us in the holidays but though he was kind it was very painful for us not to be going to our mother when everybody else who broke up for the holidays was going home.

"Because the convent was such a traumatic place we looked forward all the more to the warmth of home which was so often denied us as kids. But it made us the strong people we are now, though I do still rely on my mother," she adds.

"My father is very proud of my mother—she still looks so young and beautiful even though she is nearing fifty and she has never wavered in her beliefs. She has changed the people in Brandfort completely. They call her Mama and turn to her for anything—to sort out family squabbles, in sickness, for a meal or for advice. She is a born social worker and tries to help them all.

"Though I like to think of myself as self-assured I am still dependent on my mother. I get my strength from her. She still thinks my father will come back. She has hope and confidence and she cannot afford to give way to despair as public attention is focused on her," comments Zinzi.

By 1984 Winnie had served seven years of her banishment and Nelson had been imprisoned for 22 years.

"But my banishment has had the completely opposite effect from what the government intended. They put little Brandfort right at the top of tourist attractions. In Johannesburg I was not in touch with the international community. I was at my job from 7 a.m. till 4 p.m. and went straight home to house arrest, remaining there for the rest of the night, unable to communicate with anyone except by telephone. But here people come from all over the world to little Brandfort and I get letters from far and near. Unfortunately, though, my replies to their letters seldom seem to reach their destination, no matter how innocuous they may be."

Dr Motlana, who has known Winnie for 28 years, still marvels at her spirit.

"Her politics have not changed one bit over the years but she has mellowed and she is now more controlled," he says. "And she has such panache. She won't give the government a chance to get her down. Here in Soweto, after all these years, her name and Nelson's are more than ever household words."

Suddenly, in the first half of 1984, things started to look brighter for Winnie.

In May she travelled to Pollsmoor Prison, accompanied by Zeni and Zeni's four-year-old son, to visit Nelson. Instead of being taken to the visitors' section, however, Winnie was told the commanding officer wished to see her. She was ushered, with sinking heart, into his presence.

"I was petrified. I thought Nelson must be very ill and that the commanding officer was going to break it to me gently. So you can imagine the shock and tremendous relief and euphoria when he told me I was to be allowed a contact visit and that all future visits would be the same both for me and for the relatives of Nelson's colleagues imprisoned with him.

"Mind you," she adds, quick to stand on her rights, "it is only what is due to Nelson and the other ANC leaders. Even common criminals are allowed contact visits. Nelson and all the other Grade A political prisoners in his group are entitled to this. Great as it is for us it is not a particular break-through—it is a right, not a privilege, and one we have been fighting for for some time."

Trying to control her excitement Winnie was taken to a room to await Nelson's arrival. When he was brought in he, too, had only just been told the visit was to be a contact one. After seeing his wife on all previous occasions only through a glass partition this was almost too much to believe. It was the first time they had so much as touched each other's hand in 22 years.

"We just clung to each other," says Winnie. "We were stunned and thrilled at the same time. We could hardly take it in. Nelson clutched his little grandson to his chest throughout the visit."

Back home in Brandfort there were more happy surprises. The

Methodist Church, impressed by the way Winnie ran her home clinic for years with minimal facilities, erected a building of two rooms and a bathroom between her house and garage, to be used as a proper clinic. Then Mrs Fatima Meer, Winnie's old friend with whom she had worked in the Federation of South African Women, was released from her banning order and visited Winnie in Brandfort. Appalled by the lack of facilities in Winnie's house she arranged and paid for electricity to be installed in the building. "It has made such a wonderful difference—it actually feels something like a home now," says Winnie.

Often during the years in Brandfort Winnie has spoken of her dream to establish a centre to house a children's crèche and facilities for literacy education for adults and cultural activities for the youth of the town. As a beginning she opened a children's crèche in the nearby Methodist church hall which was soon attended by 100 little toddlers. Her efforts must have impressed the authorities, for unexpectedly and unpredictably they have made available a grant of land for the building of the youth centre which is to be Winnie's next project when the money can be found.

As for her hopes for Nelson. . . . Over the years her husband, in his spare time in prison, has worked painstakingly on a present for his wife. Using grass in the traditional manner of his people he made her a tea set and tray, expertly woven. But he has been refused permission to give it to Winnie.

"I can't think why," Nelson told his wife on one of her visits. "They watched every piece as it was woven—perhaps they think there is some message in it. But never mind—I will give it to you in person on your fiftieth birthday," he added.

That will be in September 1986.

"Well," comments Winnie, "we shall see. . . ."

Epilogue

IN COMMON WITH the majority of white South Africans I lived most of my life without ever meeting a black person socially. It was all the more amazing, therefore, that when I met Winnie Mandela we established an immediate rapport or, to put it more plainly, we liked each other. We found a remarkable similarity in our impressions, sense of humour, likes and dislikes and attitude to life. And, after interviewing dozens of people of different races and backgrounds who know Winnie, I found that her magnetism seemed to have affected them all. Her spontaneous enthusiasm for life, even in the face of the most horrendous treatment, evoked widespread admiration. So did her selfless attitude, her sincerity and her natural warmth.

This, in fact, posed a problem for me. No one had a bad word to say about her yet, being human, she has faults like the rest of us. She has been accused of arrogance, yet to watch her listening with infinite patience to an old poverty-stricken man who has come to her for advice she is all quiet humility.

Another fault, though some might call it a virtue, is that she is too trusting. She is also autocratic, something that those who do not know her might resent. She often expects others to do as she says—no arguments—and she is very conscious of her position as the wife of Nelson Mandela. He and their daughters and grandchildren are always uppermost in her thoughts to the extent that some of her friends believe she has been over-protective to her children.

The security police watch her constantly—convinced there is much going on beneath the surface. But her wits are a good deal sharper than those of the men set to watch her. Their actions, far from intimidating her, serve to keep her on her toes and she is always vociferous in her protests about their behaviour and actions whenever these fall below accepted standards.

Imperious though she may be she displays none of the status-seeking, the opportunism or the quest for personal advancement that is so

179

prevalent among political figures. She is passionately committed to an ideal for which, like Nelson, she is prepared to die if need be.

In writing this biography I have sought merely to tell the personal story of a quite remarkable woman. Naturally covert activities must remain untold, for to include them could jeopardize people in South Africa today.

In her determination and fearlessness Winnie Mandela typifies the black women of South Africa who are the unsung heroines of a largely untold struggle. Yet undoubtedly she is quite exceptional, for few people anywhere could emerge unbowed, spirit unbroken, as she has done after a life of persecution.

Echo of Mandela

In silence
the distant heroes bow their
heads
the chains weigh them down
they know no laughter
retreating . . . retreating
into a mist of bloodiness
the decaying skull
of buried freedom
emits a dull echo
of cries
free me
free me
the people are calling
looking back
they see nothing but death
where is the welcome
Why the sound of tears
hammering . . . hammering
those coffins of confessions
the decaying skull
of buried freedom
emits a dull echo
of cries
free me
free me
the people are calling
tomorrow has come
the distant heroes stand above
they look down
they shake their heads
whispering . . . whispering
into ears of emptiness
the decaying skull
of buried freedom
emits a dull echo
of cries
free me
free me
the people are calling
South Africa, are you listening?

Zinzi Mandela

181